THE *N*UCLEAR *D*ELUSION

Also by George F. Kennan

American Diplomacy, 1900–1950
Realities of American Foreign Policy
Soviet-American Relations 1917–1920
Vol. I: Russia Leaves the War
Vol. II: The Decision to Intervene
Russia, the Atom, and the West
Soviet Foreign Policy, 1917–1941
Russia and the West Under Lenin and Stalin
On Dealing with the Communist World
Memoirs 1925–1950
From Prague After Munich: Diplomatic Papers 1938–1940
Democracy and the Student Left
The Marquis de Custine and His "Russia in 1839"
Memoirs 1950–1963
The Cloud of Danger: Current Realities of American
Foreign Policy
Decline of Bismarck's European Order

THE **N**UCLEAR **D**ELUSION

SOVIET-AMERICAN
RELATIONS IN
THE ATOMIC AGE

GEORGE F. KENNAN
PANTHEON BOOKS, NEW YORK

Grateful acknowledgment is made to the following for permission to reprint previously published material:

CBS News: Excerpts of a segment from "Conversations with Eric Sevareid." Copyright © 1975 by CBS Inc. All rights reserved. Originally broadcast on September 7, 1975, over the CBS Television Network as part of the "Conversations with Eric Sevareid" series. Reprinted by permission of CBS News, a Division of CBS Inc.

Encounter: Excerpt from "Urban Interview with George F. Kennan," September 1976, pp. 4, 5, and excerpts from "A Current Assessment of Soviet-American Relationships" by George F. Kennan, March 1978, pp. 8, 10–11. Reprinted by permission of *Encounter.*

Foreign Affairs: "The United States and the Soviet Union, 1917–1976" by George F. Kennan, July 1976. Copyright © 1976 by the Council on Foreign Relations, Inc. Reprinted by permission of *Foreign Affairs.*

Harcourt Brace Jovanovich, Inc. and Faber & Faber Ltd.: Poem, "Advice to a Prophet," by Richard Wilbur. Reprinted from his volume *Advice to a Prophet and Other Poems.* By permission of Harcourt Brace Jovanovich, Inc. and Faber & Faber Ltd. First published in *The New Yorker* magazine.

Harper & Row Publishers, Inc.: Excerpt from *Russia, the Atom and the West* by George F. Kennan, pp. 55–60. Copyright © 1957 by George F. Kennan. Reprinted by permission of Harper & Row Publishers, Inc.

Little, Brown & Company, and Hutchinson Publishing Group Ltd.: Excerpts from *Cloud of Danger: Current Realities of American Foreign Policy* by George F. Kennan, chapters 12 and 13, pp. 173–227. Copyright © 1977 by George F. Kennan. Reprinted by permission of Little, Brown & Company, and Hutchinson Publishing Group Ltd.

Princeton University Press: Excerpts from *Realities of American Foreign Policy* by George F. Kennan, pp. 84, 85. Copyright 1954 by Princeton University Press. Reprinted by permission of Princeton University Press.

Theology Today: "A Christian's View of the Arms Race" by George F. Kennan, *Theology Today,* July 1982. Originally delivered by George F. Kennan at Princeton Theological Seminary on April 27, 1982.

Library of Congress Cataloging in Publication Data
Kennan, George Frost, 1904–
The nuclear delusion.
1. Soviet Union—Foreign relations—United States.   2. United States—Foreign relations—Soviet Union.   3. Atomic weapons and disarmament.   I. Title.
JX1555.Z7U437   1982   327.47073   82-14111
ISBN 0-394-52946-4

Manufactured in the United States of America
987654

To Carl Marcy and Jeanne Vaughn Mattison, co-directors of the American Committee on East-West Accord, in recognition of their devoted and effective efforts on behalf of a constructive development of Soviet-American relations.

Advice to a Prophet

When you come, as you soon must, to the streets of our city,
Mad-eyed from stating the obvious,
Not proclaiming our fall but begging us
In God's name to have self-pity,

Spare us all word of the weapons, their force and range,
The long numbers that rocket the mind;
Our slow, unreckoning hearts will be left behind,
Unable to fear what is too strange.

Nor shall you scare us with talk of the death of the race.
How should we dream of this place without us?—
The sun mere fire, the leaves untroubled about us,
A stone look on the stone's face?

Speak of the world's own change. Though we cannot conceive
Of an undreamt thing, we know to our cost
How the dreamt cloud crumbles, the vines are blackened by frost,
How the view alters. We could believe,

If you told us so, that the white-tailed deer will slip
Into perfect shade, grown perfectly shy,
The lark avoid the reaches of our eye,
The jack-pine lose its knuckled grip

On the cold ledge, and every torrent burn
As Xanthus once, its gliding trout
Stunned in a twinkling. What should we be without
The dolphin's arc, the dove's return,

These things in which we have seen ourselves and spoken?
Ask us, prophet, how we shall call
Our natures forth when that live tongue is all
Dispelled, that glass obscured or broken

In which we have said the rose of our love and the clean
Horse of our courage, in which beheld
The singing locust of the soul unshelled,
And all we mean or wish to mean.

Ask us, ask us whether with the worldless rose
Our hearts shall fail us; come demanding
Whether there shall be lofty or long standing
When the bronze annals of the oak-tree close.

—Richard Wilbur

Acknowledgments

The acknowledgments to the various publishers who have given permission for these reprintings will be found in another place in this volume. It remains for me to note certain others without whose encouragement and support the volume could hardly have appeared.

The papers here reproduced are ones written over the course of some thirty years. Most of them would fall into the category of partially or wholly extracurricular contributions, superimposed on what has been a fairly intensive program of normal academic activity. It has not always been easy to separate the two categories of work; and my thanks go out to the Institute for Advanced Study for its sympathetic understanding of the problems involved and for its patience with the added demands these contributions have placed on all of us.

Another major portion of this burden has been carried by the three long-suffering secretaries—Miss Dorothy Hessman, Miss Janet Smith, and Mrs. Alvin Goodman—without whose loyal and cheerful commitment few, if any, of these contributions could have been produced at all.

Finally, I would like to express my appreciation to the co-director of the American Committee on East-West Accord, Mr. Carl Marcy, to whose interest and enthusiasm this volume owes a large part of its origins.

Contents

III.   THE NUCLEAR AGE IN CRISIS

Introduction

The appearance of this book will mark for its author (or so, at least, he hopes) the end of an epoch of some thirty-five years' duration. It has been a period during the course of which I have tried, in occasional bouts of writing or speaking for publication, to contribute wherever I could to American understanding in matters of foreign policy, particularly policy towards the Soviet Union. The documents included in this volume are meant to be a reasonably representative selection of the results of this effort.

At no time during these three-and-a-half decades did the subjects treated here constitute my principal professional preoccupation. During six of these years I was on active duty in the American Foreign Service. During the remaining period my professional dedication was that of a scholar in the field of recent diplomatic history—not that of a pundit on current affairs. These contributions were therefore, as were the many similar ones from among which these were selected, mainly the products of purely extracurricular effort. Seldom were they spontaneously motivated. Many were speeches, delivered in response to pressures to which I found it difficult, for one reason or another, not to yield. All of them, however, whether externally provoked or spontaneously engendered, reflected a strongly felt need to make available to others, for whatever they were worth, impressions and views about Soviet-American relations drawn from many years of professional preoccupation with Russia and the Soviet Union, and from a compelling sense of the immense importance of the questions at issue.

When the war in Europe came to an end in May 1945, I was serving in the capacity of deputy to Ambassador Averell Harriman, in the American Embassy at Moscow. I was already at that time greatly depressed and concerned—concerned almost to the point of despair—over what, as it seemed to me, the outcome of the war was leading to in the relationship between the Soviet Union and the Western powers. The So-

viet leaders had been permitted, with scarcely a murmur of
protest from the Western side, to extend the formal borders
of the Soviet Union far to the west along the entire line
between the Baltic and the Black seas, depriving the three
Baltic countries of their independence, picking Poland up and
moving it some two hundred miles westward at the expense of
Germany, quietly pocketing Ruthenia, and reannexing (for it
had once been included in the old Russian Empire) the province of Bessarabia. Beyond this, its troops had overrun, with
our general approval and blessing, great portions of the remainder of Eastern and Central Europe; and it was clear, to me at
least, that Moscow had every intention of organizing political
and economic life in that entire area on its own pattern and
to its own tastes. In consequence of these changes, millions of
the inhabitants of these various regions—the newly incorpo-
rated ones as well as those now militarily overrun—were being
driven out, dispossessed, penniless, and desperate, to seek new
lives in the remainder of Central and Western Europe, wherever people would receive them. All this had happened, or was
continuing to happen, without any treaty of peace, without
even anything in the nature of a proper political discussion
with the Soviet leaders. Yet all of it was, for the moment and
for the foreseeable future, irreversible. To me, this signified an
alteration of the ethnic and geopolitical arrangements of the
European continent too sudden, too massive, too unnatural,
and too little in accord with the underlying ethnic, demographic, historical, and geographic realities of the continent to
provide a stable foundation for its political future. I was unable
to imagine that what was thus coming into being, to the apparent indifference of Washington and of American opinion,
could constitute the foundation for a permanent European
peace.

Had I attempted to express these misgivings to persons in
high positions in Washington at that time, the answer—I
knew—would have been that we expected to master all these
problems by postwar collaboration with the Soviet Union, either under the peace treaties we expected soon to be signing,
or under the general aegis of the United Nations and with the

help of the various multilateral organizations (such as the
World Trade Organization or the International Monetary
Fund) which we proposed to see established. In all of this I had
no confidence whatsoever. This entire vision of the future
rested on assumptions concerning the nature of the Stalin
regime which I knew to be unrealistic and misconceived.

What, in these circumstances, was to be done? For the long
run no hopeful solution was visible. It was all a bad show. But
it was idle, as everyone with any depth of diplomatic experience
knew, to try to look too far into any political future. The best
one could hope to do would be to find some sort of provisorium
which could keep things quiet over the immediate postwar
period and would allow for gradual change thereafter. For this,
two things were necessary. One would first have to deprive
both sides of their respective unrealistic hopes: the Russians,
of their hopes for some sort of political conquest over the
remainder of Europe in the wake of what they supposed would
be unilateral withdrawal of American armed forces from the
continent; the Americans, of their fatuous dreams of a happy
and chummy collaboration with Moscow in the restoration of
prosperity and stability throughout Europe, along liberal lines.
Once this was done, and once a reasonably realistic sphere-of-
influence arrangement had been arrived at for the European
continent, based generally on the high-water marks of the
military advance of the respective armies at the close of the
war, then, perhaps, it might eventually be possible to work out
something like a mutual withdrawal of the Russian and American forces, thus permitting the emergence of a new and independent European community, preferably under French
leadership—a community which then, over the course of the
years, might draw gradually into its fold, in ways not threatening or provocative to the Russians, not just a neutralized and
demilitarized Germany but even, eventually, the countries of
Russian-overrun Eastern and Central Europe. This, in any
case, was the most hopeful scenario that I personally was capable of imagining.

The thought never entered my head at that time that any
of these problems could be, or needed to be, solved by war.

There was no danger of anything of that sort. The Russians were profoundly war-weary. They had the most urgent need to reconstruct their war-ravaged economy. No one who had known war as they had known it in those past four years would ever wish to repeat the experience. The danger was not that of a possible Russian military onslaught on Western Europe. That was not the problem. What was needed first of all was the restoration of the economic life, the morale, and the political vigor and self-confidence of the European countries not under Soviet domination. When that had been achieved, and when it had been demonstrated to the Soviet leaders that they had exhausted their possibilities for further expansion of their dominant political influence through penetration of the Western political establishments, then the time would be ripe for negotiations looking to the total military evacuation of the continent by the Soviet and American forces.

I was not, as of 1945, in a position to write anything for publication; and there was little I could do to influence my own government behind the scenes. I did indeed write two or three confidential papers for inner-governmental consumption, trying to explain why we could not hope to have, in the postwar period, the sort of intimate collaboration with Moscow that we appeared to be dreaming about. These papers glided without perceptible effect off the slippery back of Washington's official consciousness. But the next year I followed these up with the so-called long telegram of February 1946, which did indeed, to my amazement, produce the most vigorous sort of response. A year later, by permission of the Department of State, I published the well-known "X article," making many of the same points. These pieces, together with other forces militating for a more sober view of Stalin's Russia, largely did the trick so far as curing Washington of a naïve optimism was concerned. And immediately thereafter, pleased with this success, I was happy to have a hand in turning to the second, and more constructive, task: helping General Marshall to design the program of European reconstruction that came to bear, deservedly and permanently, his name. So effective, psychologically and politically, was the Marshall Plan approach that by the beginning of 1948, when the details of the program of European reconstruction were only just being finalized, I had the impression that the first two stages of my own private scenario—the dissipation of unreal dreams of collaboration on the Western side and of unreal hopes for political triumphs on the Soviet one—had been substantially completed. The time, I naïvely supposed, was now coming for the approach—slow, gradual and circumspect, to be sure—to the third stage, that of negotiation.

It was, however, at this point that my troubles and the surprises really began. In the first six months of 1948, I discovered to my consternation and amazement that the Western Europeans, who were doing just beautifully and promised to do better still under the reassuring influence of the Marshall Plan, had suddenly decided that economic construction was not what they most needed; that their greatest danger was that of an emerging Russian military superiority in Central Europe. The Soviet leaders played into these attitudes, of course, by their failure to demobilize, as the Western Allies had done, in the immediate post-hostilities period. In the light of these anxieties, it was decided that the main thrust of Western policy must now be the creation of a military alliance directed against the Soviet Union. The United States government amiably assented, and took the lead in organizing the alliance.

From that moment on, things moved with great rapidity. Gone, now, was all serious thought of a negotiated political solution to the problems of the continent. We now had, to the relief of many people, a new military opponent. Instead of having to pursue complicated political solutions, we could now comfortably revert to the familiar patterns of old-fashioned military rivalry, only trying this time to be better prepared than we had been on the earlier occasions to confront this supposedly aggressive opponent. And events continued to further these tendencies. The shock of the first Soviet explosion of a nuclear device, in 1949, stimulated the American decision to develop the hydrogen bomb, and shifted the main burden of the conceptual defense of Europe from conventional to nuclear weapons. When, then, the Korean War broke out in 1950, this was widely accepted, by a Western community already conditioned to see the East-West differences in a purely military context, as only the first step in a great Soviet-military onslaught against what was beginning to be called "the free world." This sparked a new and greatly intensified American program of military expansion. And in line with the widespread impression that the greatest danger now facing the West was a determination of the Soviet government to expand its power —everywhere—by force of arms (an impression I did not share), the fateful decision was taken to rearm the newly created West German government and to accept it as a party to the North Atlantic Treaty Organization.

I was disheartened by these developments. I questioned their necessity. I could perceive in them only a dreadful narrowing of the possibilities for a peaceful removal of the essentially dangerous division of the European continent.

It was in those same immediate postwar years that the shadow of the nuclear arms race began to grow upon the horizon. I was obliged to confront it, for the first time, as a deputy commandant of the National War College in the first year (1946–1947) of its existence, with particular responsibility for designing the political-military course of instruction. Among the four civilian instructors then teaching at the college was Bernard Brodie, who had just edited the pioneering work on the significance of what was then called the "atomic bomb"—*The Absolute Weapon: Atomic Power and World Order.* The subject, obviously, could not be ignored. But in my lectures and discussions at the college, I found myself instinctively rejecting the suggestion that the nuclear weapon should ever again play a serious part in American strategy. I viewed its recent use against Japan as a regrettable extremism, born of the bad precedent of the conventional strategic bombings of the war just then ended and of the military fixations to which that war had conduced. Having lived through a considerable number of those "conventional" bombings, I had some idea of what they were; and I did not regard them as a justifiable expedient under the normal laws of war still theoretically in effect, nor as a particularly successful one. These attitudes, held even with relation to the non-nuclear bombings, seemed to me doubly forceful when applied to the prospect of further "atomic" ones.

Our government had, of course, at that time a monopoly on nuclear weapons. We in the State Department did not know —until 1949—just when the Russians would succeed in developing their own. We assumed that they eventually would do so. We underestimated, though not by much, the time it would take them to accomplish this task. But the possiblity—or probability—that they would someday have the same sort of weapon had little effect on my own rejection of it as a possible instrument of American military policy. If we should retain the monopoly of it, or as long as we did, I considered the device one we ought never again to use, or even to plan to use. If the Russians too came into possession of it, then it had to be viewed as a suicidal weapon, devoid of rational application in warfare; in which case we ought to seek its earliest possible elimination from all national arsenals. If we were successful in achieving its elimination, fine. If not, then we might, I thought, have to hold a few of these devices for the unlikely event that others should one day be tempted to use them against us. But we should do nothing to encourage their adoption into national arsenals anywhere. And above all, we should not design our own military forces in any way that predicated, and was dependent upon, their use.

I am free to admit that these reactions were more instinctively than rationally arrived at. It seemed to me that these so-called weapons, if introduced into our armed forces and those of other powers, and if allowed to play a part in military plans and concepts, would throw a hopeless confusion into the entire subject of military defense. Sensing this, I deplored, as I say, all talk about them. I would like to have seen it accepted that their invention and their use against Japan had been a regrettable abnormality in the development of modern concepts of warfare—a one-time misunderstanding which, we had to hope, would never be repeated. I hoped that departing from this recognition we would put the whole subject as far as possible out of mind and out of military planning, doing all in our power to encourage other governments to do likewise.

I was never called upon to take an official position on these matters until shortly after the first Soviet detonation of a nuclear device became known, in 1949. It was soon after this that the question arose whether our government should proceed to the development of the hydrogen bomb. I was then just completing a three-year period of service as director of the Policy Planning Staff of the Department of State; and I placed my views on this question before Secretary of State Dean Acheson in a paper of January 1950. I consider this in retrospect the most important paper, in its implications, that I ever wrote; and the thoughts it set forth have been basic to my attitude towards the nuclear weapons problem ever since.

A portion of the paper in question is reproduced below (pp. 3–6). That we had to hold in our arsenals a few such weapons now that the Russians were presumably acquiring them, and so long as there was no international agreement looking to their banning and elimination, I conceded. But how were we to view them? That was the crucial question. Were they to be seen as "an integral and vitally important component of our military strength, which we would expect to employ deliberately, immediately, and unhesitatingly in the event that we became involved in a military conflict with the Soviet Union"? Or were we holding them solely as a deterrent? In this last case, we must take care, I wrote, "not to build up a reliance upon them in our military planning." Our public position should then be that

> we deplore the existence and abhor the use of these weapons; that we have no intention of initiating their use against anyone; that we would use them only with the greatest of reluctance and only if this were forced upon us by methods of warfare used against us or our allies. . . .

We would, in other words, eschew the first use of such weapons ourselves; and we would try to inculcate into others the assumption that they would never again be used.

I left no doubt in Mr. Acheson's mind as to which of these alternatives I favored. If we were to adopt the first alternative —if, that is, we were to base our military strategy upon the use of nuclear weapons—then, I wrote, it would be hard "to keep them in their proper place as an instrument of national policy." Their peculiar psychological overtones would render them "top-heavy" for the purpose in question. They would impart "a certain eccentricity" to our military planning. They would eventually confuse our people, and would carry us "towards the misuse and dissipation of our national strength." Before launching ourselves on this path we should, in any case, make another effort to see whether some sort of international control could not be devised and agreed upon by the international community.

These views did not commend themselves to the secretary of state or to anyone else in the government, except Robert Oppenheimer, who joined me (for somewhat different reasons) in trying to persuade our government to pause at this particular brink. The decision to proceed with the development of the hydrogen bomb was soon taken. And this failure was one of a number of frustrations contributing to my departure from governmental service very soon thereafter.

The view that I had expressed to Mr. Acheson was further expressed and developed, however, in two public lecture series delivered in the remaining years of the 1950s, after my departure from government. First, there were the Stafford Little Lectures, delivered at Princeton in 1954.* Then, in 1957, there were the annual Reith Lectures—six of them—delivered on the Sunday evening programs of the BBC, in London.† Excerpts of these lectures also appear in this volume. In part, they represented attempts to bring before the public the view of nuclear weaponry already so decisively rejected by the United States government.

This effort, too, could hardly be called a success. The Princeton lectures, although well attended, attracted little attention outside the lecture hall. And the BBC talks, although listened to by millions of people and widely reported and discussed in

---

*George F. Kennan, *Realities of American Policy* (Princeton, N.J.: Princeton University Press, 1954).
†George F. Kennan, *Russia, the Atom, and the West* (London: Oxford University Press, 1958).

the press, encountered a violently adverse official reaction, particularly in Germany and the United States.

It was, actually, not so much the nuclear issue that produced
this negative reaction as the final plea, advanced in these same
lectures, for a political and military disengagement in Europe.
I had proposed a withdrawal of the Soviet and American armed
forces and the unification of Germany on the basis of a political
neutralization and extensive demilitarization of that country.
I had done this because I had little confidence in the permanent viability of the existing division of the continent. It allowed no proper place for the city of Berlin; nor did it offer any
hopeful solution to what must someday, I thought, be the
needs of the Eastern European countries, if and when they
succeeded in extracting themselves from an unnatural Soviet
hegemony. I still entertain these misgivings, and consider that
their validity is now being demonstrated in the case of Poland,
which the Russians are unlikely to release from its present
bondage so long as there is no other place for it to go than into
an alliance directed against the Soviet Union.

But these suggestions aroused nothing other than alarm and
indignation in Western Europe. The French and British, as
their response made clear, feared a united Germany, even a
neutralized and demilitarized one, more than they did the
Soviet military presence in the heart of Europe. The continued
division of Germany and the continent appeared to them as
the most comfortable solution for the present, whatever its
limitations for the more distant future.

By 1958, therefore, I found myself obliged to recognize the
decisive rejection of both the causes I had pursued up to that
time: the elimination of the nuclear weapon as a factor in the
military postures of the great powers, and the defusing of the
Soviet-American confrontation by the creation of an independent European "third force" to stand between them. In the
face of these reverses, there was little left for me to do but (to
use the elegant French description of retirement) to return *à
mes chères études;* and this, over the remainder of the 1950s,
the ensuing 1960s, and the early 1970s, I largely did.

I say "largely," because there were still the usual demands for speeches, interviews, and articles. Not all of these could be resisted; nor could some of them be met without the discussion of current problems. The result was a series of occasional statements, most of which eventually found their way into print. The old issues were of course, at least for the time being, exhausted. But one could still continue to tilt, where occasion presented itself, against those particular misunderstandings that heightened the dangers of Europe's divided state; and this I tried to do. I hacked away, on these various occasions, at the familiar points of confusion: nuclear blackmail; "Finlandization"; Soviet "adventurism"; the reality of Soviet aims for world conquest; the double standard applied to Soviet actions and our own; the relationship of the Soviet "threat" to our own problems of human decadence and environmental deterioration. I tried, too, to show that this Soviet threat looked less dramatic when viewed from a historical perspective than when that perspective was absent. All these efforts, of course, invited charges of naivety on my part in the face of Soviet evil intentions and other iniquities, real or supposed; and these charges, too, had from time to time (and unnecessarily, I thought) to be wearily rebutted. It was with such efforts, usually hastily sandwiched in between the more serious and time-consuming requirements of historical scholarship, that the years in question wore away. (Some of the results are presented in the second portion of the materials printed below.) Perhaps someday some patient historian—if historians there be in the planet of the future—will find himself in a position to assess their usefulness.

The year 1973 seemed to mark the beginning of a strange but greatly significant change in the official American concept of the East-West conflict. It was a change in the direction of a much more alarmed and hostile attitude towards the Soviet Union, a frame of mind in which the Soviet Union appeared in a far more menacing posture than had been the case for the past decade and in which the entire concept of the Soviet-American relationship took on an increasingly military coloration. This tendency, first observable in the early 1970s, continued to grow over the ensuing years, at least in official American opinion, finding its apotheosis in the period of the Reagan administration, when it attained the quality of a full-fledged war scare, accompanied by a high degree of general anti-Soviet hysteria.

I found this development at the time, and continue to find it today, both puzzling and alarming. That tendencies of this nature should make themselves felt at the time in question was not in itself what amazed me. Such tendencies had been present ever since the Korean War. Every president since Harry Truman had been, to one degree or another, intimidated by them. What amazed me was that they should have reappeared in such strength just in 1973, at a time when the various faults of the Soviet regime as seen from Washington were certainly no worse than they had been at any other time in the sixty years of its existence, at a time when Soviet fortunes were in the guiding hands of the outstandingly cautious and unadventuresome Brezhnev, and at a time when Messrs. Nixon and Kissinger had just demonstrated the existence of certain possibilities—limited, of course, but not negligible—for an East-West relationship based on something less than total military confrontation.

Recognizing that many intelligent and honorable people, some of them my good friends, were among the proponents of this new belligerency, I tried to understand the reasons they gave for it.

One of the reasons given was that Moscow was continuing to oppose causes and regimes we supported in the Third World. This, in the words of people who had seen nothing adventuristic in our own involvements in Vietnam or in Iran, was called "Soviet adventurism."

It was hard for me to see why these Soviet activities should either surprise us or alarm us. The Russians had tried time and again, in the course of the Nixon-Kissinger exchanges, to warn us that "détente" could not, in their view, be taken to extend to what they called the "ideological" conflicts—meaning the various rivalries for influence in the Third World. Nor were

Soviet efforts along these lines, so far as I could see, any more far-reaching or, above all, any more successful than those they had put forward in earlier decades. The Russians, plainly, were not very good colonialists or neo-colonialists—worse, if anything, than we were. The attitudes of the Third World regimes towards both the superpowers were generally cynical and exploitative. Those regimes would obviously take what they could get from each of us; but I saw small danger of their falling under the extensive influence of either.

Another reason offered for reaccentuation of Cold War rhetoric and behavior was that Moscow was not adhering to the various documents (they were not exactly obligations) signed in 1975 at Helsinki. For this argument, too, I found it hard to develop enthusiasm. Ever since the Yalta Conference, I had argued against the usefulness (and indeed had emphasized the danger) of asking Moscow to sign up to declarations of high and noble principle. I had tried to point out that words meant different things to the Soviet leaders than they did to us, and that it was better, in dealing with them, to stick to strictly specific agreements which left aside all questions of motive and purported only to specify what each of us would do, when we would do it, and under what conditions it would be done. A large part of the Helsinki undertakings flew in the face of these warnings; as a result of which I had viewed the whole Helsinki process, at the time, as a great mistake, likely (as proved to be the case) to complicate East-West relations rather than to improve them.

But the reason most commonly offered, and most vociferously asserted, for these latter-day transports of militant anti-Sovietism was that the Soviet leaders, in the post-Vietnam years, when the development of the American armed forces was essentially stagnating, had continued, steadily and relentlessly, to develop their own.

There was something to this argument. The Soviet leaders would indeed have been well advised to temper their efforts along these lines, during the years in question, or at least to give better explanations for their failure to do so. But here again, I could not go along with much of what was now the American conventional wisdom. These Soviet leaders had never given us reason to believe that "détente" meant that they would unilaterally moderate their armament efforts in the absence of specific bilateral agreements for action in the field of arms reduction. And it was we, not they, after all, who failed to ratify the only agreement for the control of nuclear weapons—the second SALT Treaty—that was negotiated in those very years. I saw ample evidence that the Russians were trying to catch up with us in the development of long-range nuclear weaponry; I saw no signs, and no reason to suppose, that they intended to go beyond a general state of equivalence.

Nor could I find, even after long hours of poring over the bulletins of the London Institute for Strategic Studies, that the development of the Soviet conventional armed forces, particularly in the European theater, was nearly as drastic or as frightening as was suggested by the bits of statistical information regularly leaked by the Pentagon to the American press. If indeed the statistical balance between their forces and ours was developing to our disfavor, I was inclined to see the causes of this as much in our own neglect—in our uncontrolled inflation and in the great wastefulness of our military establishment—as in any sinister Soviet designs for the launching of World War III.

Observing then, in the years of the late 1970s and early 1980s, the seemingly inexorable advance of this hysteria of professed fear of and hostility to the Soviet Union, but finding so little objective reason for it, I could only suspect that its origins were primarily subjective; and this seemed to me to suggest something much more sinister than mere intellectual error: namely, a subconscious need on the part of a great many people for an external enemy—an enemy against whom frustrations could be vented, an enemy who could serve as a convenient target for the externalization of evil, an enemy in whose allegedly inhuman wickedness one could see the reflection of one's own exceptional virtue. Perhaps all this was not unnatural in the light of the frustrations and failures American society had been suffering at that time: such things as Vietnam; the inexplicable student rebellion; the hostage crisis; inflation; growing and uncontrollable crime and pervasive corruption

and cynicism of every sort in our own country; a feeling that
the development of our society was out of control. But such
states of mind, more often subconscious than consciously experienced, were powerful and insidious ones. They offered
great temptations to the politician anxious to avoid involvement
with the bitter internal issues of the day and eager to reap,
instead, the easy acclamations usually produced in our society
by a vigorous ringing of the chauvinist bell. And the moods
that they produced—the sweeping militarization of the American view of East-West differences; the assumption of deadly
and irreconcilable conflict; the acceptance of the likelihood, if
not the inevitability, of a Soviet-American war; the contemptuous neglect of the more favorable possibilities—these, and the
official behavior that flowed from them in the halls of government, seemed to me to represent a situation of immense,
immediate, and—what was most tragic—quite unnecessary
danger.

All this would have been bad enough in any case. I had seen
two world wars fought in my lifetime. A possible third one
appeared to me as something perilously close to the final catastrophe, even without the nuclear weapon. But this was also a
time when the Soviet and American nuclear arsenals were
growing to wholly monstrous and nightmarish dimensions, in
a process to which there appeared to be no plausible ending.
I had never regarded the SALT process as a hopeful way of
mastering the nuclear problem. It seemed clear to me that the
pace of technological innovation in the weapons field far out-
stripped the pace of the SALT-type negotiations, so that their
results tended regularly to be outdated before they were even
arrived at. I had always thought, and had made attempts to
persuade the Kennedy administration, that only a series of
prearranged bold unilateral but reciprocal measures of restraint
could have any serious prospects of mastering this problem.
Now, especially with the failure of the United States government to ratify the last SALT accord, the situation seemed truly
serious. Had the unrestrained competition in the development
of nuclear weaponry not been accompanied by the new wave
of hysteria in the interpretation of Soviet intentions generally,

it might have been somewhat less menacing—though not much. But combined with the officially promoted view that the Soviet leaders were little else than a latter-day replica of the German Nazis, that they were pursuing intensive and relentless plans for military conquest in every direction, and that this, and nothing less, was the real problem we faced in our relations with them—this view, combined with the nuclear weapons race, now wholly out of control, seemed to present dangers without precedent in human history, a real and imminent threat to everything that one valued, beginning with the safety and future of one's own children.

In these circumstances, and again responding to invitations that seemed to present favorable occasions for such statements, I spoke publicly several times on these subjects in the years 1980 and 1981—spoke, I may say, with a new earnestness and sense of urgency, both about the nuclear danger and about the view of the Soviet Union by which our military policies were inspired. The record of those statements constitutes the final part of the documents printed in this volume.

Looking back over the efforts represented by all these documents, one would have to recognize that they have been for the most part failures. The nuclear arsenals have reached the fantastic dimensions just noted; and there is no reason to suppose that they will do anything other, in the coming period, than continue to grow. And relations with the Soviet Union have now deteriorated to a point where, to read the official statements emanating from Washington, one would suppose we were already in a state of undeclared war—an undeclared war pursued in anticipation of an outright one now regarded as inevitable.

The failure is not total. So far as the nuclear weapon is concerned, there has been an encouraging public response to the pleas, my own and those of many others, for a reversal of the weapons race. The NATO governments most intimately concerned with the problems in question have not yet responded to such suggestions, to be sure, with anything other than consternation and indignant rejection. But the dangers and the political sterility of a defense posture based extensively

on nuclear weaponry are so glaringly obvious, and are now
becoming visible to so many people everywhere, that even the
governments, one must suppose, will ultimately have to take
account of them, unless war intervenes before that fortunate
moment arrives.

When it comes to Soviet-American relations a different
situation—alas—prevails. Here, the oversimplifications would
appear to have triumphed. The attendant distortions of understanding are so deeply planted in the public mind, in this
country and elsewhere, that one despairs of their early correction. Great masses of people in this country and in Europe have
now been taught to believe that the Soviet leadership has been
obsessed, ever since World War II, with a desire to invade
Western Europe, and has been "deterred" (gnashing its teeth,
we must suppose, in frustration) only by the threat of nuclear
retaliation. A variation of this supposed verity, very common
in Western Germany, is the belief that the Soviet side, in the
event that the threat of a nuclear response were to be removed,
would not at once attack but would subject the Western European NATO countries to various forms of nuclear blackmail,
in the face of which those countries, confronted with an overwhelming Soviet superiority in conventional strength, would
have no choice but to "surrender." A subsidiary myth, equally
widely believed, is that the Soviet superiority in conventional
armed strength in Central Europe has been remorselessly growing and has now reached such vast dimensions that there is no
way the NATO powers could conceivably match it.

All of these assumptions and scenarios are either quite incor-
rect or highly improbable; but they are now so deeply and
widely implanted in the public mind that in all probability
nothing I could say, and nothing any other private person could
say, could eradicate them. Only a senior statesman and political
leader, speaking from the prominence and authority of high
governmental position (in our country, a president, presumably) could have a chance of re-educating the public successfully
on these various points, and this is something for which one
sees, at this present juncture, not the slightest prospect.

Meanwhile, we face the fact (and it is here that the greatest
danger comes in) that distortions of this nature, like all false

prophecies and all false images of conflict and enmity, tend to be self-fulfilling. As this volume makes clear, I have personally never seen the evidence that the Soviet leaders seriously considered attacking Western Europe at any time in these postwar years. It has seemed to me evident that there were many considerations of self-interest that militated against even the contemplation by them of any such undertaking. This conclusion was based, however, on the assumption that they did not see the outbreak of another great war as unavoidable, and imminent, from causes outside their own control.

Today, I would not know where all this stands. The Soviet leaders cannot, I am sure, suspect NATO of any plans for the deliberate inauguration of hostilities in the European theater. No coalition of democratic governments, as they must well know, would be capable of anything like that. But wars, as they are also aware, do not always arise from acts of outright aggression; they are more apt to proceed, as history shows, from confused situations arising against a background of extreme political tension. For years now, American governmental figures have talked and acted as though the balance of military power was the only significant factor determining the future of Soviet-American relations. In deference to what would appear to be this assumption, endless calls have gone out for accelerated military preparations on the part of the United States and its NATO allies. In deference to the same assumption (or if not, what else?) strenuous efforts have been made, including elaborate approaches to China, to enlist all the countries around the Asiatic borders of the Soviet Union in a single pattern of political-military encirclement of that country. For years now, American public discussions of military problems have usually been cast, often from the lips of senior governmental figures, in the most open terms of an envisaged Soviet-American military confrontation, as though this were the only type of armed conflict anyone would be capable of imagining, and as though it were in the imminence of such a conflict that we saw "the present danger."

What impression must all this make upon the persons charged with the ultimate powers of decision in Moscow? Are we sure we know? We do not, at the moment, in this period

of instability and transition in the composition of the supreme
Soviet organs of power, even know exactly who these people
are, or what their capacities are for sober and realistic judgment
of external phenomena. What we do know is that Russian
officials, and Soviet officials above all, have always been prone
to exaggerated suspicions. More than once in the history of
Soviet power, they have thought to see signs of aggressive
intent on the part of others where no such intent was actually
present. It is, I suppose, barely possible that these men, or those
who will soon replace them, reading the belligerent statements
of some of the men around President Reagan, observing the
travels and pronouncements of his secretary of defense, and
noting the various military documents regularly leaked to the
press by the Pentagon and White House staff, will arrive at the
comforting conclusion that this is all just television-screen post-
uring before the American public; that the endless debates and
calculations of the military think-tanks about what we could do
to the Russians and what they could do to us represent no more
than empty exercises in scholastic pedantry; that our professions of determination to grind the Russians into the dust
economically and to exploit their resulting misery reflect no
seriously hostile intention but are only some harmless form of
domestic-political horseplay. This is, as I say, possible; but it is
not probable. It seems to me more probable that the new
Soviet leaders will see sinister motives behind these various
phenomena—that they will conclude, in particular, that we
have come to see war as inevitable and have put out of our
minds all possibilities for the peaceful accommodation of our
differences. If they gain this impression, then they, too, will
tend to put such possibilities out of theirs. And if this is the
point they arrive at, then all the reassuring things I have had
to say about Soviet intentions in the statements adduced
below, and elsewhere, become questionable. If Moscow is
brought to see a war as both unavoidable and imminent, then,
so far as I am concerned, all bets are off. Then anything could
happen.

Before terminating these observations, I have one confession to make. There is need for it here, because the state of

mind it reveals is of recent origin, and is not reflected in the documents here reproduced.

In all these expressions of opinion I have been going on the assumption that while another conventional war in Europe would indeed be an immense danger, not to be undergone without new and lasting damage to European civilization, nevertheless the main and most urgent necessity was to get rid of the nuclear weapons, the mere extensive existence of which, given the possibilities for error and accident, presented a danger beyond any other that civilized life had ever known; and that, having got rid of these latter, one could somehow set out with good confidence to muddle along with the conventional weapons, hoping that some sort of balance among them could eventually be achieved and that they, too, would never come into use. But I had always resisted the suggestion that war, as a phenomenon of international life, could be totally ruled out, partly because the demands for the outlawing of war were usually cast (like the pathetically unrealistic Kellogg Pact) in universal and therefore wholly impractical terms, partly because it was so hard to see what other ultimate sanction for the protection of national interest could be devised.

I am now bound to say that while the earliest possible elimination of nuclear weaponry is of no less vital importance in my eyes than it ever was, this would not be enough, in itself, to give Western civilization even an adequate chance of survival. War itself, as a means of settling differences at least between the great industrial powers, will have to be in some way ruled out; and with it there will have to be dismantled (for without this the whole outlawing of war would be futile) the greater part of the vast military establishments now maintained with a view to the possibility that war might take place. The reasons for this conclusion are multiple; but among them are, first, the recognition that the weapons of this age—even the so-called conventional ones—are of such destructiveness that there can be no clear line between the discriminate ones and the weapons of mass destruction; and second, the similar recognition that so extensively has public understanding and official habit been debauched by the constant encouragement given it to perceive the military balance primarily in nuclear terms that it would probably be incapable of making these fine distinctions between one kind of weapon and the other in time of war, and the use of the immensely destructive "conventional" weapons would in all probability slip over into the use of those to which the term "conventional" could not properly be applied.

No one could be more aware than I am of the difficulty of ruling out war among great states. It is not possible to write any sure prescription as to how this might be achieved, particularly because the course of international life is not, and cannot be, determined over the long term by specific treaties or charters agreed upon at a single moment in history and reflecting only the outlooks and circumstances of that particular moment. It is the ingrained habits and assumptions of men, and above all of men in government, which alone can guarantee any enduring state of peaceful relations among nations.

One thing, however, is certain: namely, that without frank, searching, and patient communication among governing figures, and without understandings of such moment that they would effectively rule out not only the very thought of war but also the preparations for it, the establishment of new habits and assumptions among men is never going to be achieved.

It is, so far as the nongovernmental observer can ascertain, many years (if ever) since anything resembling a real, intimate, and useful political communication between the Soviet and American governments has taken place. The ingrained procedures of both governments make this difficult. It will not be achieved by summit meetings, under the glare of publicity, nor indeed by any exchanges that take place before the eys or the ears of the world public. And it will not be successful unless it is based on a recognition of the perceived security interests of both partners (even those for which the other partner may have small sympathy), and unless it rules out extraneous issues and sticks strictly to the question as to how those security interests can find dependable mutual recognition in a world devoid of the massive military sanction. And the most difficult task of all will be that which confronts any American statesman who undertakes to conduct such discussions: how, namely, to make their results intelligible and acceptable to an American public confused by the many past appeals to its emotions, unaccustomed to being asked to confront soberly a series of highly complex realities, and informed primarily by commercial media of information whose dedication is to the oversimplification and dramatization of reality rather than the education of the public to the recognition of its bitter complexities.

The achievement, however, of these formidable tasks of statesmanship—this, and not just the elimination of nuclear weaponry—is what it will take to assure to Western civilization a reasonable chance of survival in the face of the tremendous dangers with which it is today confronted.

1

THE NUCLEAR PROBLEM IN ITS INFANCY

1 EARLY REFLECTIONS ON THE ATOMIC BOMB

*The Atomic Bomb and
the Choices for American Policy*
(1950)

The problem whether it is desirable for this government to move now as far as possible and as rapidly as possible towards international control is only part of a deeper problem, involving certain very far-reaching judgments and decisions of national policy, both foreign and domestic. It is not the purpose of this paper to deal exhaustively with this deeper problem or to make recommendations for its solution. But it is important, in any consideration of the international control problem, to identify the larger problem of which it is a part, to see what other things are logically involved in it, and to note certain factors bearing upon it which have particular importance from the standpoint of international control.

The real problem at issue, in determining what we should do at this juncture with respect to international control, is the problem of our attitude towards weapons of mass destruction in general, and the role which we allot to these weapons in our own military planning. Here, the crucial question is: Are we to rely upon weapons of mass destruction as an integral and vitally important component of our military strength, which we would expect to employ deliberately, immediately, and unhesitatingly in the event that we become involved in a military conflict with the Soviet Union? Or are we to retain such weapons in our national arsenal only as a deterrent to the use of similar weapons against ourselves or our allies and as a possible means of retaliation in case they are used? According to the way this question is answered, a whole series of decisions are influenced, of which the decision as to what to do about the international control of atomic energy and the prohibition of the weapon is only one.

We must note, by way of clarification of this question, that barring some system of international control and prohibition of atomic weapons, it is not questioned that *some* weapons of mass destruction must be retained in the national arsenal for purposes of deterrence and retaliation. The problem is: for what purpose, and against the background of what subjective attitude, are we to develop such weapons and to train our forces in their use?

We may regard them as something vital to our conduct of a future war—as something without which our war plans would be emasculated and ineffective—as something which we have resolved, in the face of all the moral and other factors concerned, to employ forthwith and unhesitatingly at the outset of any great military conflict. In this case, we should take the consequences of that decision now, and we should obviously keep away from any program of international dealings which would bring us closer to the possibility of agreement on international control and prohibition of the atomic weapon.

Or we may regard them as something superfluous to our basic military posture—as something which we are compelled to hold against the possibility that they might be used by our opponents. In this case, of course, we take care not to build up a reliance upon them in our military planning. Since they then represent only a burdensome expenditure of funds and effort, we hold only the minimum required for the deterrent-retaliatory purpose. And we are at liberty, if we so desire, to make it our objective to divest ourselves of this minimum at the earliest moment by achieving a scheme of international control.

We should remember that more depends on this basic decision than simply our stance towards the problems of international control. It must also have an important effect on our
domestic atomic-energy program, and particularly on what we
do about the superbomb. If we decide to hold weapons of mass
destruction only for deterrent-retaliatory purposes, then the
limit on the number and power of the weapons we should hold
is governed by our estimate as to what it would take to make
attack on this country or its allies by weapons of mass destruction a risky, probably unprofitable, and therefore irrational
undertaking for any adversary. In these circumstances, the
problem whether to develop the superbomb and other weapons
of mass destruction becomes only a question of the extent to
which they would be needed to achieve this purpose. It might
be, for example, that the present and prospective stockpile of
conventional bombs, combined with present and prospective
possibilities for delivery, would be found adequate to this purpose and that anything further in the way of mass-destruction
weapons would be redundant, or would fall into an area of
diminishing returns.*

If, on the other hand, we are resolved to use weapons of mass
destruction deliberately and prior to their use against us or our
allies, in a future war, then our purpose is presumably to inflict
maximum destruction on the forces, population, and territory
of the enemy, with the least expenditure of effort, in full
acceptance of the attendant risk of retaliation against us, and
in the face of all moral and political considerations. In this case,
the only limitations on the number and power of mass-destruction weapons which we would wish to develop would presumably be those of ordinary military economy, such as cost, effi-
ciency, and ease of delivery.

Depending, therefore, on which of these courses is selected,

*Note that the Soviets claim that their aim in developing the bomb is only to have
"enough" for purposes of retaliation. Vishinsky, in his speech before the United
Nations Assembly on November 10, 1949, said: "We in the Soviet Union are utilizing
atomic energy, but not in order to stockpile atomic bombs—although I am convinced
that if, unfortunately and to our great regret, this were necessary, we should have as
many of these as we need—no more and no less."

our decision on the superbomb might be one of two diametri-
cally opposite ones. (*Foreign Relations of the United States* 1.)

The Nuclear Deterrent and the
Principle of "First Use"
(1954)

The weapons of mass destruction have to be borne in mind
as one of the great and sorry realities of our day. We cannot
rule out the possibility of war, for wars can arise from many
constellations of circumstance; and similarly we cannot rule out
the possibility that these horrible weapons may someday be
used. For this contingency we must make the most realistic
dispositions we can, but we must not be carried away by these
dispositions to the point where we neglect the cultivation of
the other possibilities. There is also the possibility that there
will be no general war. And there is always the further possibility that even if there is a war, it may prove the part of prudence
for us all to restrict ourselves either to the more conventional
weapons or to a more conventional use of the unconventional
ones. For this, too, we must be prepared. It is for this reason
that I would fail to comprehend any policy that did not preserve a balance between conventional weapons and the weapons of mass destruction, and especially one that staked our
world position on the power of weapons we ourselves, in the
final event, might or might not find it prudent to use. The
sooner we can learn to cultivate the weapons of mass destruction solely for their deterrent value, the sooner we can get away
from what is called the principle of "first use" of such weapons,
the sooner we can free ourselves from the false mathematics
involved in the assumption that security is a matter of the
number of people you can kill with a single weapon, the better
off, in my opinion, we will be. (*Realities of American Policy.*)

A Sterile and Hopeless Weapon
(1958)

The beginning of understanding rests, in this appalling
problem, with the recognition that the weapon of mass de-

struction is a sterile and hopeless weapon which may for a time serve as an answer of sorts to itself and as an uncertain sort of shield against utter cataclysm, but which cannot in any way serve the purposes of a constructive and hopeful foreign policy. The true end of political action is, after all, to affect the deeper convictions of men; this the atomic bomb cannot do. The suicidal nature of this weapon renders it unsuitable both as a sanction of diplomacy and as the basis of an alliance. Such a weapon is simply not one with which one can usefully support political desiderata; nor is it one with which one readily springs to the defense of one's friends. There can be no coherent relations between such a weapon and the normal objects of national policy. A defense posture built around a weapon suicidal in its implications can serve in the long run only to paralyze national policy, to undermine alliances, and to drive everyone deeper and deeper into the hopeless exertions of the weapons race.

Now these thoughts are not mine alone. They are shared by many other people. They have been well expressed on other occasions. If I have seen fit to restate them here, it is to make clear my own position and to emphasize that their validity is in no way affected by the Soviet earth satellite, nor will it be affected if we launch a satellite ourselves.

But even among those who would go along with all that I have just said, there have recently been other tendencies of thought with which I also find myself in respectful but earnest disagreement. I have in mind here, in particular, the belief that the so-called tactical atomic weapon—the atomic weapon designed, that is, to be used at relatively short range against the armed forces of the adversary, rather than at long range and against his homeland—provides a suitable escape from the sterility of any military doctrine based on the long-range weapon of mass destruction.

Let me explain what I mean. A number of thoughtful people, recognizing the bankruptcy of the hydrogen bomb and the long-range missile as the bases for a defense policy, have pleaded for the simultaneous cultivation of other and more discriminate forms of military strength, and ones that could conceivably be used for some worthwhile limited national objective, and without suicidal effect. Some have advocated a policy of what they call "graduated deterrents." Others have chosen to speak of the cultivation of the capacity for the waging of "limited war," by which they mean a war limited both in the scope of its objects and in the destructiveness of the weapons to be employed. In both instances what they have had in mind was to find an alternative to the hydrogen bomb as the basis for national defense.

One can, I think, have only sympathy and respect for this trend of thought. It certainly runs in the right direction. Force is, and always will be, an indispensable ingredient in human affairs; the alternative to a hopeless kind of force is never no-force-at-all. A first step away from the horrors of the atom must be the adequate development of agencies of force more flexible, more discriminate, and less suicidal in their effects. Had it been possible to develop such agencies in a form clearly distinguishable from the atomic weapon, this unquestionably would have provided the most natural path of escape from our present dilemma.

Unfortunately, this seems no longer to be an alternative, at least so far as the great nuclear powers are concerned. The so-called tactical atomic weapon is now being introduced into the armed forces of the United States, and there is an intention, as I understand it, to introduce it into Great Britain. We must assume that the same thing is occurring in the Soviet Union. While many people in our respective governments have become convinced, I am sure, of the need for being able to fight limited as well as total wars, it is largely by the use of the tactical atomic weapon that they propose to fight them. It appears to be their hope that by cultivation of this tactical weapon we can place ourselves in a position to defend the NATO countries successfully without resorting to the long-range strategic one; that our adversaries can also be brought to refrain from employing the long-range one; that warfare can thus be restricted to whatever the tactical weapon implies; and that in this way the more apocalyptic effects of nuclear warfare may be avoided.

It is this thesis which I cannot accept. That it would prove possible, in the event of an atomic war, to arrive at some tacit and workable understanding with the adversary as to the degree of destructiveness of the weapons that would be used, and the sort of target to which they would be directed, seems to me a very slender and wishful hope indeed.

But beyond this, let us bear in mind the probable ulterior effects—the effects, particularly, on the people in whose country such a war might be waged—of the use of tactical atomic weapons. There seems to be a cheerful assumption that these weapons are relatively harmless things, to be used solely against the armed forces of the enemy and without serious ulterior disadvantages. But surely this is not so! Even the tactical atomic weapon is destructive to a degree that sickens the imagination. If the experience of this century has taught us anything, it is that the long-term effects of modern war are by no means governed just by the formal outcome of the struggle in terms of victory or defeat. Modern war is not just an instrument of policy. It is an experience in itself. It does things to him who practices it, irrespective of whether he wins or loses. Can we really suppose that poor old Europe, so deeply and insidiously weakened by the ulterior effects of the two previous wars of this century, could stand another and even more horrible ordeal of this nature? Let us by all means think for once not just in the mathematics of destruction—not just in these grisly equations of probable military casualties—let us rather think of people as they are: of the limits of their strength, their hope, their capacity for suffering, their capacity for believing in the future. And let us ask ourselves in all seriousness how much worth saving is going to be saved if war now rages for the third time in a half-century over the face of Europe, and this time in a form vastly more destructive than anything ever known before.

Unfortunately, the danger is not even limited to the possible effects of the use of the tactical atomic weapon by our own English or American forces in time of war. There is a further contingent danger, and a very imminent one as things now stand; and this is that atomic weapons, strategic or tactical or both, may be placed in the arsenals of our continental allies as well.

I cannot overemphasize the fatefulness of such a step. I do

not see how it could fail to produce a serious increase in the existing military tension in Europe. It would be bound to raise a grave problem for the Russians in respect of their own military dispositions and their relations with the other Warsaw Pact countries. It would inevitably bring about a further complication of the German and satellite problems. Moscow is not going to be inclined to entrust its satellites with full control over such weapons. If, therefore, the Western continental countries are to be armed with them, any Russian withdrawal from Central and Eastern Europe may become unthinkable once and for all, for reasons of sheer military prudence regardless of what the major Western powers might be prepared to do.

In addition to this, it is perfectly obvious that the larger the number of hands into which the control over atomic weapons is placed, the smaller will be the possibility for their eventual exclusion from national arsenals by international agreement, and the more difficult it will be to preclude complications of all sorts. So long as only three great powers are involved, there is at least a chance that things can be kept under control. To place these weapons in the hands of a number of further countries is practically to assure that there can in future be no minor difficulty in Europe that does not at once develop into a major one.

I am aware that similar warnings against the introduction of the atomic weapon into the armaments of the continental countries have also recently been part of the stock in trade of Soviet diplomacy. I cannot know what the motives of the Soviet government have been in taking this position. I certainly cannot say that they have all been ones we could respect. But I think we must beware of rejecting ideas just because they happen to coincide with ones put forward on the other side. Moscow says many harmful and foolish things; but it would be wrong to assume that its utterances never happen to accord with the dictates of sobriety and good sense. The Russians are not always wrong, any more than we are always right. Our task, in any case, is to make up our minds independently. (*Russia, the Atom and the West.*)

2

EAST-WEST RELATIONS UNDER THE SHADOW OF THE NUCLEAR BOMB

2

THE AMERICAN-SOVIET RELATIONSHIP: A RETROSPECTIVE

(1976)

When, in the year 1917, Russian society was overtaken by the most tremendous and far-reaching upheaval it had ever known, American opinion makers were poorly prepared to understand either the meaning or the implications of this event.

This was partly because there was little understanding in the United States of that day for Russian history or for the nature of the political society in which these events were taking place. Russian studies had been developed in North America only on the tiniest and most rudimentary of scales. Knowledge of Russia rested on the tales of the occasional traveler or on the reports of press correspondents, very few of whom were qualified to see deeply into the great political and social stirrings that tormented the life of Russia in those final decades of tsardom. The traditional antipathy of Americans for the tsarist autocracy was understandable enough; but it was seldom balanced by any realistic examination of the nature of the possible alternatives. And in the final years before World War I, governmental and journalistic opinion in the United States had tended to be pre-empted by the problem of the treatment of Jews within the Russian Empire, to the detriment of the attention given to other and even deeper aspects of the slow crisis in which Russian society was then embraced.

This was the situation as of 1914. But as the First World

War ran its course, and particularly in the year 1917, there
came to be imposed upon this general shallowness of understanding a far more serious source of confusion: and that was
America's own involvement in the war. If it be conceded that
one of the most stubbornly ingrained characteristics of American democracy has been its inability to accept and experience
military involvement without becoming seriously disoriented
by it and without permitting it to distort judgment on other
questions of policy, then it must be said that never did this
weakness reveal itself more sharply and fatefully than in American outlooks on Russia during the First World War. Entering
the war only a few weeks after the first of the two Russian
revolutions of 1917, Americans resolutely declined, from that
time on, to view Russian developments from any standpoint
other than that of the war against Germany, and not of a
thoughtful and objective image of that war, at that, but rather
as it was perceived through the grotesquely distorting lenses of
wartime propaganda and hysteria.

Thus both Russian revolutions of that fateful year were
seriously misperceived. The first—the fall, that is, of tsardom
and its replacement by a regime which was liberal-democratic
at least in intent—was welcomed less in its possible significance
for the future of Russia than because it was seen—wholly
incorrectly—as releasing forces of enthusiasm for the war effort
previously suppressed by a supposedly pro-German imperial
court. The second revolution, in November, which brought the
Bolsheviks to power, was misunderstood by reason of the widespread belief that the Bolshevik leaders were German agents;
as a result of which the new regime, not generally expected to
last very long in any case, was opposed less for what it really
was than out of resentment for its action in taking Russia out
of the war.

It was only after the termination of hostilities against Germany that the way was cleared, in theory at least, for a view
of Russian communism as a political phenomenon in its own
right. But by this time a new welter of bewildering and misleading factors had entered in: such things as the passions and
uncertainties of the Russian civil war; the exaggerations of

propaganda on both sides; our own semi-involvement in the Allied intervention; and the measures of the new Communist regime with relation to tsarist debts and foreign property. It was not really until the early 1920s, after the termination of the Russian civil war and the overcoming of the famine of 1921–1922, that the meaning of what had occurred in Russia since 1917 began to emerge from the turmoil of events with sufficient clarity to permit the beginnings of thoughtful and reasonably informed debate in the United States over the nature of the problem which the installment of Lenin and his associates in the traditional seats of Russian power presented for American statesmanship.

II

Before going on to consider the nature of this problem and of the responses with which it met, it would be well to have a glance at one particular involvement of the United States which occurred in the confusion of those immediate postrevolutionary years and the main effect of which was to muddy the waters of mutual understanding for decades to come. This was America's part in the Allied intervention of 1918–1920. Precisely because this action has so often been depicted by Soviet propagandists as an unsuccessful effort by the American government to unseat the Soviet regime, it is important to recognize its essential origins and dimensions.

The United States sent troops only to two areas of Russia: to the European north, in the neighborhood of Arkhangelsk on the White Sea, and to eastern Siberia. Both of these areas were far from the main theaters of the Russian civil war then in progress. In neither case was the decision to dispatch these troops taken gladly or—one may say—independently, in Washington. In neither case was it motivated by an intention that these forces should be employed with a view to unseating the Soviet government. In neither case would the decision have been taken except in conjunction with the world war then in progress, and for purposes related primarily to the prosecution of that war.

First—as to northern Russia. President Wilson consented to
the dispatch of American forces to that region only in the face
of a massive misunderstanding on his part of the situation
prevailing there, only with great misgivings and skepticism as
to the usefulness of the undertaking, and only when it had been
insistently urged upon him by the British and French, with the
support of Marshal Foch, then Supreme Allied Commander in
Europe, all of whom portrayed it as a measure required by the
war effort against Germany. What brought him to the decision
was well described by his secretary of war, Newton Baker, in
a letter written some years later. He had convinced the president, Baker wrote, that the decision was unwise,

> but he told me that he felt obliged to do it anyhow because the
> British and French were pressing it upon his attention so hard
> and he had refused so many of their requests that they were
> beginning to feel that he was not a good associate, much less
> a good ally.

The three battalions of American troops (for that is all it
amounted to) were sent to Arkhangelsk, and served there,
under British command. The decisions as to how and for what
purposes they should be employed were British decisions, not
American ones. The uses to which they were put were ones of
which Wilson was ignorant at the time, ones he had never
envisaged, ones of which, had he known of them, he would
unquestionably have disapproved. That the units remained
there after the end of the war with Germany was due to the
fact that they were held there, over the winter of 1918–1919,
by the frozen condition of the White Sea. When the ice broke
up, they were removed as soon as this could be accomplished.

As for the troops that were sent to Siberia: the consent to
the dispatch of these units was given only when Wilson's
unwillingness to send them had been worn down by six months
of pleading from the Western Allies. Their missions were restricted to the guarding of the Suchan coal mines, in the
Maritime Province, and of certain sections of the Trans-
Siberian Railroad north of Manchuria—services, that is, that

were of high importance to the lives and comfort of the inhabitants of the region, regardless of politics. The areas in question were, at the time of the dispatch of the units, thousands of miles removed from the main theaters of the Russian civil war; and the units took no part in that war. Their presence probably gave some satisfaction and comfort to the non-Bolshevik Russian forces in Siberia (although little love was lost between those forces and the Americans), and it may have had some effect in delaying the eventual extension and consolidation of Bolshevik power in the area. But this, so far as Wilson's intentions were concerned, was incidental. That they remained as long as they did, and were not withdrawn in 1919, was due to suspicion of the Japanese (who also had troops in the area) on the part of the Americans rather than to hostility towards the Bolsheviks.

The task of attempting to understand the permanent elements of the Soviet-American relationship will be best served if these regrettable episodes of the final weeks and immediate aftermath of the First World War be left aside, as the pathetic by-products of wartime confusion, weariness, and myopia that they really were, and the focus of attention be shifted to the more enduring sources of conflict that were destined to complicate the relationship over ensuing decades.

III

The first and most fundamental of these sources of conflict was, of course, the ideological commitment of the Bolshevik-Communist leadership. This was something wholly new in the experience of American statesmanship. It was the manifestation of a form of hostility Americans had never previously encountered. Americans had known, of course, the phenomenon of war, as a situation defined and recognized by international law. But war was (normally) the expression of a hostility limited both in time and in intent. It was limited in time because it was coincidental with the existence of a formal state of war. It was limited in intent because the aims it was designed to serve were normally ones of a limited nature: the transfer of a province from one sovereignty to another; a change in the arrangements governing maritime commerce; the replacement of one ruler by another for dynastic reasons.

But what American statesmen now saw themselves faced with, in the person of the new Russian Communist regime, was something quite different: a governing faction, installed in the seats of power in another great country, which had not even dreamed of declaring war formally on the United States but which was nevertheless committed, by its deepest beliefs and by its very view of its place in history, to a program aimed at the overthrow of the entire political and social system traditional to American society—committed, that is, to a program calculated to inflict upon the society of the United States a damage more monstrous in the eyes of most Americans than any they might expect to suffer from even the worst of purely military defeats at the hands of the traditional sort of adversary.

This situation was destined to undergo many changes and modifications in the course of the ensuing decades. There would be times when the ideological hostility on which it was based would be soft-pedaled for reasons of tactical expediency. In general, the cutting edge of the hostility would be progressively blunted over the course of the decades by the erosion of frustration and the buffeting of contrary events; so that it would come, with the years, to assert itself more as a rhetorical exercise than as a guide to policy. Particularly with respect to the United States, where its chances for political success were singularly slender, this messianic dedication would gradually lose its bite with the passage of the years, so that Americans would ultimately come to fear it less for its possible effect upon themselves than for its effect on other peoples: its effect, that is, in alienating those peoples from that portion of the international community with which America could have a comfortable and friendly relationship and adding them to that other sector (to be greatly increased in the Third World after World War II) in which America, and all that she stood for, would be regarded only with prejudice, misunderstanding, and rejection.

But these would be gradual changes. They lay, as of the early

1920s, well in the future. They were not yet generally visible or predictable. The American statesmen of that day had to take the ideological challenge at its own words, and deal with it accordingly.

It would be wrong, of course, to suppose that this sort of hostility remained one-sided, or even that it was wholly one-sided from the start. It naturally bred its own reaction on the part of many Americans; and it would be idle to pretend that this reaction was always thoughtful, reasonable, devoid of prejudice, sensitively responsive to the nature of the challenge itself. It was a reaction that would manifest itself, down through the years, in many ways, most of them unpleasant: in the anti-Red hysterias of 1919–1920 and 1950–1953; in the vulnerability of large sections of the American public to the sanguine urgings of the Chinese Nationalist and "captive nations" lobbies; in the exaggerated military apprehensions and phantasmagoria of the post–World War II period. Hampering at every turn the development of a sound and effective response to the challenge which had provoked it (or provided the rationalization for it), this exaggerated reaction would constitute at all times a complication of the Soviet-American relationship in its own right. And it was not slow in making itself felt in the immediate aftermath of the Revolution. It was one with which American policymakers were obliged to contend from the start, in their efforts to design an effective response to the challenge in question.

Before proceeding to examine this response, it would be well to note that there were two features of this unprecedented relationship that were fated to constitute basic and unalterable elements of the problem it presented for American statesmanship. One was the fact that, fiery as were the assertions of intent upon the part of this ideological opponent to destroy *our* system, and heartily as this challenge was accepted by sections of our own public opinion, neither side was in a position, or ever would be in a position, to achieve the total destruction of the other. Each might hope for it; each might do what little it could to abet processes that seemed to run in that direction. But neither could, by its own action, achieve it; nor did ulterior forces produce this result. The result was that each had to accept, for better or for worse, the other's existence and to start from there in the designing of policy.

This "peaceful coexistence"—if you will—was a reality of the relationship from the beginning. It did not need a Khrushchev or a Brezhnev to discover it or create it.

The other inalterable element of this problem, destined to become wholly visible and compelling only in later years but also present, in reality, from the start, was the fact that in this complicated world of ours there could be no international relationship which was one of total antagonism or total identity of interests—none which did not contain both sorts of ingredients, however uneven the mix. Just as there could be no relationship of friendship undiluted by elements of rivalry and conflict, so there could be no relationship of antagonism not complicated by elements of occasional common purpose or desiderata.

The fact that these *were*, precisely, the basic elements of the problem was not always clearly visible to all the American statesmen who had to deal with it, any more than it was to all sections of American private opinion. But the fact was always there, on the visible surface or below it; and those who attempted to ignore it risked the prospect of being yanked back sooner or later, and sometimes in painful ways, to the plane of reality.

IV

It would be unfair to search in actions of the American statesmen in the 1917–1920 period for the elements of a serious and considered response to this problem. The situation was too chaotic, their oversight over events too imperfect, for this to be expected of them. But with the end of Allied intervention, and with the gradual grinding to a halt of civil conflict in Russia, the situation became clearer; and it is instructive to observe the emergence of a more systematic and principled response.

The first to make the attempt to design such a response were those who were responsible for the conduct of American diplomacy at the end of the Wilson administration.

These did not really include Wilson himself, except as the influence of his thinking from earlier days still made itself felt. He lay, at that time, ill and helpless in the White House. But it was impossible for his assistants not to take some attitude towards the problem, and this they proceeded to do. It was a purely ideological attitude, as uncompromising in its acceptance of the Bolshevik challenge as were the authors of that challenge in their creation of it. It was succinctly expressed in the note that Secretary of State Bainbridge Colby addressed to the Italian government on August 10, 1920. "It is not possible for the Government of the United States," Colby wrote,

> to recognize the present rulers of Russia as a government with which the relations common to friendly governments can be maintained. This conviction has nothing to do with any particular political or social structure which the Russian people themselves may see fit to embrace. It rests upon a wholly different set of facts.
>
>   . . . Upon numerous occasions the responsible spokesmen of this Power . . . have declared that it is their understanding that the very existence of Bolshevism in Russia, the maintenance of their own rule, depends, and must continue to depend, upon the occurrence of revolutions in all other great civilized nations, including the United States, which will overthrow and destroy their governments and set up Bolshevist rule in their stead.
>   . . . We cannot recognize, hold official relations with, or give friendly reception to the agents of a government which is determined and bound to conspire against our institutions.

The essential features of this response are easily observed. It accepted the first of the elements of the problem noted above: the existence of the Soviet state and the impossibility, for the United States, of doing anything to change that situation, beyond the refusal to accord formal diplomatic recognition. It revealed no awareness of the second element: namely, the existence of a limited area of common interest; indeed, its authors would have been skeptical of the thesis that such an area existed, or could exist. Nothing of this nature was visible to them.

This declaration was, of course, one of the swan songs of the Democratic administration of that day. That administration shortly was to be replaced by the first of the successive Republican administrations of Harding, Coolidge, and Hoover.

The Republicans accepted the reasoning of the Colby note, as far as it went; but to the motivation of the policy of non-recognition they added one more feature not present in Mr. Colby's pronouncement. This was a reference to the failure of the Soviet government to recognize any obligation in principle to assume the foreign debts of previous Russian regimes or to reimburse foreigners for property previously owned by them in Russia and now nationalized by the Soviet authorities. In the view of these Republican statesmen, the Soviet government, in order to regularize its relations with the United States, would not only have to cease its advocacy of revolution in the United States and its ill-concealed support for elements working to that end, but would have to assume the financial obligations incurred by previous Russian regimes to the United States government and to American nationals.

On this, the relationship rested for thirteen years. Individual American businessmen were not prevented from traveling in Russia and trading with the Soviet foreign-trade monopoly, at their own risk. Herbert Hoover, emerging with halos of glory from his leadership of the American relief effort in Europe at the end of the war, was not prevented from organizing and conducting in Russia, in 1921–1922, as a private undertaking, the magnificent work of the American Relief Administration, which saved several million people from starvation and may well, for all anyone can tell, have saved the Soviet regime itself from utter failure and collapse. But the American government itself was officially blind to a regime whose attitude and behavior it found unacceptable as a basis for formal relations.

The Soviet government, for its part, was quite aware, over the years in question, of the complexity of its relations with the Western countries, and of its need for certain forms of collaboration with them even in the face of ideological hostility. It did not, however, find itself too adversely affected by the American stance. What it wanted from the Western powers was trade, recognition, and credit. Trade it got, without difficulty, from all of them, including even the United States. Recognition it received, mostly in the years 1924–1925, from all the leading European powers. Commercial credit, too, it succeeded in obtaining from some of them, notably the Germans, within the relatively narrow limits prescribed by circumstances. All these benefits were achieved without paying the price the United States government was demanding: which was the suppression of the Comintern and the sort of activity its existence implied, as well as major concessions in the field of debts and claims. Thus the incentive on the part of the Soviet leaders to meet these American demands became weaker with the passage of the years. They wanted American recognition and financial help; but they were not prepared to pay, and did not need to pay, the price the Republican administrations of 1921–1933 were demanding.

V

Franklin Roosevelt's assumption of the presidency in 1933, marked, of course, a fundamental turning point in the relationship. To him, the old question of debts and claims seemed, in itself, unimportant, likewise the issue of propaganda. He recognized that these issues engaged the feelings and interests of important segments of American opinion, and thus presented domestic-political problems he would have to meet; but he could not have cared less about them from his own concept of America's external interests.

On the other hand he was, in contrast to his Republican predecessors, very conscious indeed of the existence of at least one area of common interest with the Soviet Union: with relation, namely, to the threat of Japanese penetration into the mainland of Asia. This was shortly to be supplemented by similar feelings on his part with relation to Hitler's obvious intention to win for Germany a dominant position on the European continent.

Franklin Roosevelt was contemptuous from the start of the reasoning of the State Department and of the upper-class Eastern establishment which had for so long inspired Republican policy towards Russia. He was much influenced by Mr. William C. Bullitt, the brilliant and charming dilettante who, as a very young man, had been sent to Russia in 1919, during the Peace Conference, by Lloyd George and Colonel House, and had returned convinced that it *was* possible to deal with Lenin and his associates and disgusted with the Allied leaders for declining to do so. FDR, persuaded as he was of his own great powers of ingratiation and persuasiveness, readily lent his ear to Mr. Bullitt's suggestions that the Soviet leaders, being human, would now be responsive to a more friendly and conciliatory approach, and that, having even more to fear than did the Americans from a Japanese penetration into Manchuria (not to mention an expansion of Nazi power into Eastern Europe), they could easily be made into an asset from the standpoint of possible resistance to these developments. And the result, of course, was the re-establishment of diplomatic relations between the two countries in the autumn of 1933.

It was characteristic of FDR that the preliminary Soviet-American agreements (the so-called Roosevelt-Litvinov letters), on the basis of which the establishment of diplomatic relations was arranged, were ones designed, in his own eyes, not at all to assure to the United States any real advantage in the forthcoming official relationship, but rather to meet the prejudices and disarm the criticisms of groups within the American political community whose opposition to recognition was to be expected. Such of the wording of the Litvinov letters as appeared to assure a cessation of subversive propaganda and activity with relation to the United States, and a settlement of the questions of debts and claims, was thus far too vague and full of loopholes to satisfy anyone really wishing to see these issues resolved; and in this sense it could be charged, and was, that Roosevelt's acceptance of it constituted a direct misleading of the American public. But there is no reason to suppose that FDR doubted that desirable results could be obtained in the end, by one means or another, regardless of the precision of the language of the understandings. For real gains in the Soviet-American relationship the president was inclined to rely, not on written documents, but on the power of his own charismatic personality.

The result, for anyone who knew anything about Russia, was predictable. The issues of debts and claims were never resolved; it remained for the passage of time to drain them of most of their meaning. The propaganda and the support for subversion did not cease. Trade, instead of increasing, declined. The Soviet authorities, recognition having now been obtained, the Japanese threat having for the moment slightly abated, and it having become clear that in any case the Americans were not going to fight the Japanese for their benefit, now lost interest either in making good on the concessions they had semipromised or in making new ones. The new American Embassy in Moscow, founded initially with exuberant optimism under the auspices of Mr. Bullitt as the first ambassador, soon fell victim to the age-old Russian aversion to dealing with the resident diplomat (regarded as too *avisé*, too guarded and skeptical, too patient, and too little susceptible to being rushed into hasty agreements) and its preference for dealing directly with the foreign statesman innocent of any close personal knowledge of Russian realities.

So Mr. Bullitt, not surprisingly, left in disgust after a year or so of frustration, to join at a later date the ranks of the Soviet Union's most bitter critics and opponents on the Washington scene. His successor, Mr. Joseph E. Davies, a man to whom for various reasons the appearances of good relations were more important than their reality, made a valiant attempt, if not a very plausible one, to maintain those appearances. But he, too, soon gave up the struggle, and retired from the Russian scene in 1938. The American Embassy was felt, thereafter, to share for years to come the dim semi-existence customarily led by the Moscow diplomatic corps, isolated, guarded, seen but not heard, useful—in this case—primarily as a school for young Russian-speaking diplomats, obliged to contemplate and to study the Russian scene while they pondered the reasons for their own isolation.

The years immediately following the resumption of Soviet-American relations were, of course, the years of the purges. With the millions that perished in those fearful agonies, there perished also—there could not help but perish—the magical afterglow of the hope and idealism of the Lenin period. By the end of the 1930s not even the greatest enthusiast could ignore the dread hand of terror, denunciation, and moral corruption that had gripped Russian society. Only the most wishful and uninstructed of foreign sympathizers, outraged by the phenomenon of European fascism and inclined to give the benefit of the doubt to anything that even appeared to oppose it, could retain the illusion that here was a superior and more humane civilization.

But such sympathizers did, of course, exist in the United States. They were encouraged by what seemed to them to be the implications of the economic crisis that had now overtaken their own "capitalist" country. They encouraged, and helped to preserve, in Franklin Roosevelt and certain of those around him a somewhat battered but undefeated partiality for the Soviet regime: a readiness to dismiss the tales of the horror and injustice of the purges as just some more of the anti-Soviet propaganda that had been pouring out from reactionary circles ever since the Revolution, and a readiness to continue to believe in the essential progressiveness of the Soviet "experiment"—all the more acceptable, seemingly, by way of contrast to the European fascism and Japanese militarism just then advancing upon the world scene.

The Nazi-Soviet Non-Aggression Pact of 1939 was of course a great blow to people who held these views. Together with the ensuing Russian attack on Finland and taking over of the Baltic states, this unexpected development was enough to suppress down to the year 1941 the latent pro-Sovietism just described. But it was not a mortal blow. The inclinations in question survived, below the surface, into the eventful year of 1941. And when in June of that year Russia herself was invaded by Hitler, it was as if the unhappy events of 1939–1940 had never occurred: Robert Sherwood's moving play on the suffering of the Finns under the Russian attack was soon revised with the replacement of the Finns by the Greeks, and the Russians by the Germans. A new era, once again dominated by the fact of America's being at war, was beginning to dawn in the history of Soviet-American relations.

VI

Never, surely, has the congenital subjectivity of the American perception of the outside world been more strikingly illustrated than in the change of attitude towards Russia that followed Pearl Harbor and the ensuing German declaration of war on the United States, in December 1941. Gone, as if by magic, were most of the memories and impressions of the past. Forgotten, now, were the Russian purges, along with the reflection that the men now running Russia's war effort and diplomacy were the same who had once conducted those bloody persecutions. Forgotten, too, were the cruelties only recently perpetrated by Beria's police establishment upon the innocent populations of eastern Poland and the Baltic states. Forgotten was the fact that Russia's involvement in the war was neither the doing nor the preference of her own rulers: that, on the contrary, they had made desperate efforts to remain aloof from it, and would, had this been possible, have witnessed without a quiver of regret further Western reverses in the war, provided only that the contest was sufficiently bloody and prolonged to exhaust Germany's war-making potential along with that of its Western opponents. Ignored, in large measure, was the fact that the demands which Stalin was making on his Western allies, even as early as the end of 1941, were substantially the same as those he had placed before Hitler as the price for Russia's initial neutrality. In place of all this there emerged, and was systematically cultivated in Washington, the image of a great Soviet people, animated by the same noble impulses of humane indignation and yearning for a future free of all tyranny by which Americans conceived themselves and their allies to be animated, fighting with inspiring heroism and grandeur against an opponent in whose repulsive political personality all the evil of an imperfect world seemed to be concentrated.

The image was, of course, not wholly wrong. The heroism was there. So was the grandeur of the effort. That the Western powers owed their military victory to that effort, in the sense that without it their victory could never have been achieved, was undeniable. It was also true that a great proportion of the Soviet people conceived themselves to be fighting for the defense of their homeland—an aim with which Americans could at least sympathize even if the homeland was not theirs.

But what was important, of course, in the given circumstances, was not what the mass of the Soviet people conceived themselves to be fighting for but what their rulers perceived as the uses they wished to make of victory; and this, as the past had shown, was a different thing.

Weighty reasons were offered for the idealization of the Soviet ally, and the encouragement of belief in the possibilities of postwar collaboration with it, that inspired so much of Franklin Roosevelt's wartime policy. Without a belief on the part of the public that Russians and Americans were fighting for the same thing it would have been impossible, it was said, to maintain American enthusiasm for the war effort and the readiness to give aid to Russia in the pursuit of that effort. Without American aid, without American moral support, without expressions of American confidence in Russia, Stalin might have been tempted, it was argued, to make a compromise peace with the Nazis, permitting Hitler to concentrate his entire great force against the West.

There was much in these arguments. The weakest part of them was perhaps that which most appealed to the American military establishment, now the center of American policymaking: the fear of a complete Russian collapse or (as the tide turned) of a separate Russian-German peace. Stalin, of course, would have loved the latter, though not until the Germans had been expelled from at least the pre-1939 territory of the Soviet Union; and once things had gone that far, and the Germans had begun to crumble, then his own appetite was stimulated to a point where he saw no need to stop. But that fear of such a development, coupled with a sense of humiliation over their own inability (until 1944) to pick up a larger share of the military load, haunted the American military leadership throughout the war and inclined them to give moral and material support to their Soviet opposite numbers in every possible way, is clear.

Behind this whole argument, however, there lay a deeper question: and that is whether it ever pays to mislead American opinion, to be less than honest with it, even in the interests of what is perceived by the political leadership as a worthy cause. It is characteristic of wartime psychology that the end tends to be seen as justifying the means. But when the means include the manipulation of opinion by the creation and propagation of unreal images, there is always a price to be paid at a later date; for the distortions thus engendered have someday to be straightened out again.

And so it was in the years after 1945. It must be said in defense of FDR and his associates that they probably never fully realized (although they came closest to it in the days just preceding the president's death) the extent to which they *were* actually misleading American opinion on this point. Amid the stresses of a great war effort it is particularly easy for the wish to play father to the thought. Stalin, too, encouraged, in his own delicate and cautious way, the propagation of this myth: soft-pedaling, while the war was in progress, certain forms of criticism of the Western Allies, and making adroit use of those idealistic semantic generalities which can mean all things to all people.

But the fact remains, however extenuating the circumstances, not only was the unreal dream of an intimate and happy postwar collaboration with Russia extensively peddled to large portions of the American public during the war, but they were encouraged to believe that without its successful realization there could be no peaceful and happy future at all.

The events of the final weeks of the war and of the immediate post-hostilities period rapidly demolished this dream. Event after event: the behavior of the Soviet forces in the half of Europe they overran; the growing evidence that the Soviet authorities had no intention of permitting the free play of democratic forces in the countries of that great region; their cynical reluctance to collaborate in the restoration of economic life and stability in areas they did not control; the continued secretiveness and inscrutability of Soviet policymaking and political action; the failure to enter upon any extensive demobilization of the Soviet armed forces; the narrow, suspicious, and yet greedy behavior of Soviet representatives in the new international organizations—all these things fell heavily upon a public in no way prepared for them; nor was there any Franklin Roosevelt, now, with his talent for the leadership of opinion, to make the transition in company with those whom he had, wittingly or otherwise, misled—to ease them out of the wartime euphoria he had once eased them into.

The results were not unnatural. Unrequited love now turned only too easily into unreasonable hatred. To people taught to assume that in Russian-American postwar collaboration lay the only assurance of future peace, the absence of that collaboration, in the light of a conflict of aims becoming daily more visible, inevitably conduced to visions of war. To people unsettled by the recent experience of being at war, the real personality of Russia, in all its vast complexity, was often lost to view; and in its place, assuming in many respects the aspect of the late-departed Hitler, there emerged one of those great and forbidding apparitions to the credence in which mass opinion is so easily swayed: a monster devoid of all humanity and of all rationality of motive, at once the embodiment and the caricature of evil, devoid of internal conflicts and problems of its own, intent only on bringing senseless destruction to the lives and hopes of others.

Neither of these reactions—neither the exorbitant wartime hopes nor the angry postwar disillusionment—were shared by all sections of American opinion; and where they were shared, not all experienced them in like degree. There were those who labored, with moderate success, to correct them. Alone, the effect of these aberrations might not have been deep or enduring. But they happened to fall in, most fatefully, with the emergence of a new pattern of fears and misunderstandings—this time of a military nature.

The failure of the Soviet government to carry out any extensive demobilization in the post-hostilities period has already been mentioned. Here again, taken outside the context of ulterior circumstances, this might not have been unduly alarming. For centuries it had been the custom of Russian rulers to maintain in being, even in time of peace, ground forces larger than anyone else could see the necessity for. The reasons for this must be assumed to have been primarily of a domestic political and social nature. But this time the circumstances— and along with the circumstances, the reactions—were different in a number of respects.

In the first place, in contrast to the situation of earlier decades and centuries, the Russian armed forces now had an area of deployment in the very heart of Europe, with secure lines of support and communication behind them. In the past, it had been possible to employ their great numerical strength in Western Europe only after first overcoming both the geographic and the military impediments of the territory that lay between Russia's traditional western borders and the industrial heartland of the European continent. Now, a Soviet offensive, if one wished to launch one, could be started from within 60 miles of Hamburg or 100 miles of the Rhine. To military planners, trained to give greater weight to capabilities than to intentions, this could not fail to be disturbing. And not to military planners alone. The peoples of Western Europe, all of whose memories, with one or two exceptions, included the overrunning of their homelands by foreign troops at one time or another, and usually within the past century, suffered from *la manie d'invasion* and found it difficult to believe that the Russians, having already overrun so many countries since 1944, should not wish to overrun more.

Secondly, Western strategists, inclined anyway, for reasons of professional prudence and others, to a chronic overrating of the adversary's capabilities, now found themselves confronting no longer the traditional primitive and slow-moving Russian ground forces, defensively strong on their own ground but not well fitted for offensive purposes against a strong Western opponent, but rather, modern, mechanized units with equipment little inferior, sometimes not inferior at all, to that of the

Western armies themselves. The result, of course, was increased anxiety.

But overshadowing both of these factors, as a source for the
militarization of American thinking about the problem of relations with Russia, was, of course, the development by the
Russians of a nuclear capability, visible from 1949 onward.

The writer of these lines knows no reason to suppose that
the Soviet leadership of Stalin's day ever allotted to the nuclear
weapon anything resembling a primary role in its political-
strategic concepts. There is no reason to doubt that Stalin saw
this weapon as he himself described it: as something with
which one frightened people with weak nerves. Not only was
he aware from the start of its potentially suicidal quality, but
he will be sure to have recognized, as one in whose eyes wars
were no good unless they served some political purpose, that
for such purposes the nuclear weapon was ill suited: it was too
primitive, too blindly destructive, too indiscriminate, too prone
to destroy the useful with the useless.

Merciless as he could be, and little as his purposes may have
coincided with ours, Stalin was entirely rational in his external
policies; war, for him, was not just a glorified sporting event,
with no aim other than military victory; he had no interest in
slaughtering people indiscriminately, just for the sake of
slaughtering them; he pursued well-conceived, finite purposes
related to his own security and ambitions. The nuclear weapon
could destroy people; it could not occupy territory, police it, or
organize it politically. He sanctioned its development, yes—
because others were doing so, because he did not want to be
without it, because he was well aware of the importance of the
shadows it could cast over international events by the mere fact
of its inclusion in a country's overt national arsenal.

But it was not to this weapon that he looked for the satisfaction of his aspirations on the international plane. Indeed, in
view of the physical dangers the weapon presented, and the
confusion its existence threw over certain cherished Marxist
concepts as to the way the world was supposed to work, he
probably would have been quite happy to see it removed entirely from national arsenals, including his own, if this could be

done without the acceptance of awkward forms of international inspection. And if his successors were eventually forced into a somewhat different view of the uses of the weapon, as they probably were, it was surely the Western powers, committed from the start to the first use of the weapon in any major encounter, whether or not it was used against them, that did the forcing.

Little of this was perceived, however, on the Western side —and on the American side in particular. Once again, the interest in capabilities triumphed over any evidence concerning intentions. The recognition that the Russians had the weapon, and the necessary carriers, served as sufficient basis for the assumption that they had a desire to use it and would, if not deterred, do so.

In part, this was the product of the actual discipline of peacetime military planning. The planner has to assume an adversary. In the case at hand, the Russians, being the strongest and the most rhetorically hostile, were the obvious candidates. The adversary must then be credited with the evilest of intentions. No need to ask *why* he should be moved to take certain hostile actions, or whether he would be likely to take them. That he has the capability of taking them suffices. The mere fact that they would be damaging to one's own side is regarded as adequate motive for their execution. In this way not only is there created, for planning purposes, the image of the totally inhuman and totally malevolent adversary, but this image is reconjured daily, week after week, month after month, year after year, until it takes on every feature of flesh and blood and becomes the daily companion of those who cultivate it, so that any attempt on anyone's part to deny its reality appears as an act of treason or frivolity. Thus the planner's dummy of the Soviet political personality took the place of the real thing as the image on which a great deal of American policy, and of American military effort, came to be based.

Nor does this exhaust the list of those forces which, in the aftermath of World War II, impelled large portions of influential American opinion about Russia into a new, highly militaristic, and only partially realistic mold. The fall of China to its own Communists, a development that was by no means wholly agreeable to the Soviet leadership, came soon to be regarded as the work of Moscow, implemented (was there ever an odder flight of the imagination?) not directly but through the agency of naïve or disloyal Americans. Out of this, and out of the related discovery that there was political mileage to be made by whipping up suspicions of fellow citizens, there emerged the phenomenon known as McCarthyism, the unquestioned premise of which was the existence of a diabolically clever Russian Communist enemy, consumed with deadly hostility and concerned only with our undoing. And not long thereafter came the misreading by the official Washington establishment of the nature and significance of the Korean War—a misreading by virtue of which an operation inspired overwhelmingly by local considerations related to the situation in the Manchurian-Korean area, and one from which the Soviet government studiously kept its own forces aloof, came to be regarded and discussed in Washington as, in effect, an attack by the Soviet Red Army across international borders, and as only the first move in a sort of Hitlerian "grand design" for military world conquest.

It was out of such ingredients that there emerged, in the late 1940s and early 1950s, those attitudes in American opinion that came to be associated with the term "Cold War." These were never to dominate all of American opinion. Many people, while generally prepared to give a polite show of outward credence to the image of the Soviet adversary just described, remained aware of the scantiness of their own information and were prepared, by and large, to reserve judgment. In their extreme form the fixations in question remained the property of a small but strongly committed right-wing minority, the electoral weakness of which was repeatedly demonstrated, and of the military budgeteers and nuclear strategists, who had little electoral significance at all.

Nevertheless, the image of the Soviet Union as primarily a military challenge was now widely accepted. And for reasons that warrant more scholarly investigation than they have received, the resulting fixations acquired a curiously hypnotic power over the professional political community. A certain show of bristling vigilance in the face of a supposed external danger seems to have an indispensable place in the American political personality; and for this, in the early 1950s, with Hitler now out of the way, the exaggerated image of the menacing Kremlin, thirsting and plotting for world domination, came in handy. There was, in any case, not a single administration in Washington, from that of Harry Truman on down, which, when confronted with the charge of being "soft on communism," however meaningless the phrase or weak the evidence, would not run for cover and take protective action.

These observations should not be misunderstood. The reality that deserved recognition in place of this exaggerated image was never its opposite. There were indeed, throughout this period, as there always had been before, threatening elements in both Soviet rhetoric and Soviet behavior. That behavior remained marked at all times, in one degree or another, by features—disrespect for the truth; claims to infallibility; excessive secrecy; excessive armaments; ruthless domination of satellite peoples; and repressive policies at home—that were bound to arouse distaste and resentment in American opinion, and thus to feed and sustain the distorted image of Soviet Russia we have just had occasion to note. It is not too much to say, in fact, that if the Soviet leaders did not want to live with this image, they could have done a great deal more than they actually did to disarm it; a few obviously specious peace congresses and the ritualistic repetition of professions of devotion to the cause of "peace" (as though peace were some sort of abstraction) were never enough.

Most serious of all, as distortions of understanding from the Soviet side—particularly serious because massively and deliberately cultivated—were the dense clouds of anti-American propaganda put out, day after day, month after month, and year after year, in the postwar period by a Soviet propaganda machine that had never been inhibited by any very serious concern for objective and observable truth, and was now more reckless than ever in its disregard for it. The extremes to which this effort was carried, particularly in those final months of

Stalin's life that coincided with the high point of the Korean War, were such as to be scarcely conceivable except to those who experienced them at first hand. Here, the United States was portrayed, of course, as the most imperialist, militaristic, and generally vicious of all aggressors. And this affected the climate of relations at both ends; for on the one hand, the very extremism of these attacks confirmed Americans in their view of the sinister duplicity of Soviet policy (why, it was asked, should a government that was really of peaceful intent have such need for the lie in the statement of its case?); while on the other hand, those Soviet leaders and officials who had a part in the making of policy, despite the cynicism with which they launched this propaganda, could not help being affected by it themselves, and were influenced accordingly in their interpretation of American behavior.

Against this background of mutual misunderstanding, the course of Soviet-American relations in the immediate postwar years, and to some extent down into the Khrushchev era, was determined by a series of spontaneous misinterpretations and misread signals which would have been comical had it not been so dangerous. The Marshall Plan, the preparations for the setting up of a West German government, and the first moves towards the establishment of NATO, were taken in Moscow as the beginnings of a campaign to deprive the Soviet Union of the fruits of its victory over Germany. The Soviet crackdown on Czechoslovakia and the mounting of the Berlin blockade, both essentially defensive (and partially predictable) reactions to these Western moves, were then similarly misread on the Western side. Shortly thereafter there came the crisis of the Korean War, where the Soviet attempt to employ a satellite military force in civil combat to its own advantage, by way of reaction to the American decision to establish a permanent military presence in Japan, was read in Washington as the beginning of the final Soviet push for world conquest; whereas the active American military response, provoked by this Soviet move, appeared in Moscow (and not entirely without reason) as a threat to the Soviet position both in Manchuria and in eastern Siberia.

And so it went, less intensively, to be sure, after Stalin's death, but nonetheless tragically and unnecessarily, into the respective misinterpretations of such later events as the bringing of the Germans into NATO, the launching of the first Sputnik, the decision to introduce nuclear weapons into the continental components of NATO, the second and prolonged Berlin crisis provoked by Khrushchev in the late fifties and early sixties, and finally the Cuban missile crisis. Each misreading set the stage for the next one. And with each of them, the grip of military rivalry on the minds of policymakers on both sides was tightened and made more final.

VII

One of the most fateful effects of this preoccupation with the military aspects of the relationship was to dull in a great many Americans, including many legislators, opinion-makers and policymakers, the sensitivity to real and significant changes occurring in Soviet society and leadership. Most fateful of all was their effect in obscuring the significance of Stalin's death. The changes that followed on that event were of course gradual ones, and ones of degree. In part, they were the objects of deliberate efforts at concealment on the part of the new leadership. All this, admittedly, made them not always easy of recognition. But they were important. They greatly deserved American attention. And they were not undiscernible to trained and attentive eyes, of which the American government had a number, if it had cared to use them.

The Khrushchev era, and particularly the years from 1955 to 1960, presented what was unquestionably the most favorable situation that had existed since the 1920s for an improvement of relations with Russia and for a tempering of what was by this time rapidly becoming a dangerous, expensive, and generally undesirable competition in the development of armed forces and weapons systems. Khrushchev certainly had his failings— among them, his boasting, his crudeness, his occasional brutalities, his preoccupation with Soviet prestige and his ebullient efforts to ensure it—most of these were the failings of a man

who was outstandingly a peasant *parvenu,* not born to the habit
or expectation of great power and with a tendency to overdo
in the exercise of it. But he was intensely human, even in
relations with the ideological opponent. One could talk with
him—talk, so far as he was concerned, to the very limits of
one's physical stamina (his own appeared to be unlimited).

The primitive and naïve nature of Khrushchev's faith in
Marxist-Leninist principles as he understood them was, strange
as this may seem, an advantage; for it caused him to wish, even
in confrontation with the capitalist visitor, to convince, to
convert, and—to this end—to communicate. This, from the
standpoint of efforts to reach a better understanding, was far
better than the crafty cynicism of a Stalin. To which must be
added the recollection that Khrushchev's secret speech, at the
Twentieth Congress of the Party in 1956, dealt to the extreme
Stalinist tendencies in the Party and in the world communist
movement a blow from which they were never fully to recover.

The Khrushchev period, too, was of course not lacking in
serious crises. In addition to the Berlin crisis mentioned above,
there was, above all, the Hungarian rebellion of 1956. It should
not be taken as an apology for the Soviet action at that time
if one points out that this action was neither correctly understood nor usefully reacted to on the American side. The misunderstanding arose (as it was again to do in the face of the
Czechoslovak crisis of 1968) from the apparent inability of a
great many Americans to understand that the Soviet hegemony
over Eastern Europe, established by force of arms in the final
phases of the war and tacitly accepted by this country, was a
seriously intended arrangement that the Soviet leadership proposed to maintain, if necessary, by the same means with which
they had acquired it.

As for the American reaction: the resort to armed force by
the Western powers was never a feasible alternative; the conflict could not have been limited; and even Hungary was not
worth a nuclear war. Where the United States might usefully
have acted was by an offer to make certain modifications in its
military posture in Western Europe if the Soviet government
would let things in Hungary take their course. But the preoccu-

pation of the American secretary of state at that moment with the deplorable happenings of the Suez crisis, together with the already firm commitment of the United States and the other NATO members against anything resembling a disengagement in Europe, made such an offer impossible.

The situation remained, therefore, essentially unchanged. In certain relatively powerless sectors of the American government establishment, people continued to explore, patiently and with insight, the possible channels of approach to a less dangerous and more hopeful state of affairs. But in other and more powerful echelons, other people continued to carry on with the concepts born of the Korean War, as though Stalin had never died, as though no changes had occurred, as though the problem were still, and solely, the achievement of superiority in preparation for a future military encounter accepted as inevitable, rather than the avoidance of a disastrous encounter for which there was no logical reason at all and in which no one could expect to win. The interests of the gathering of military intelligence continued to be given precedence over the possibilities for diplomatic communication. And who does not remember the result? The almost predictable accident occurred. The U-2 plane was brought crashing to the ground in the center of Russia, carrying with it the prestige of Khrushchev, discrediting him in the eyes of his own colleagues, shattering his ascendancy over the Soviet military establishment, hastening the end of a career already seriously jeopardized by other factors.

VIII

Four years were still to elapse before Khrushchev's final fall —years marked by President Kennedy's rather unsuccessful effort to establish a personal relationship with Khrushchev, and by the further complication of the Cuban missile crisis. Whether the unwise effort to put missiles in Cuba was something forced upon Khrushchev by his own colleagues, or whether it was a last desperate gamble on his part with a view to restoring his waning authority, seems still to be uncertain;

but that it completed the destruction of his career is not. And from 1965 on, with Lyndon Johnson now in the White House by his own right and with Khrushchev removed from the scene, a new period opened in Soviet-American relations.

The omens, at the outset of Mr. Johnson's incumbency, were not, by and large, wholly unfavorable. The shock of the recent unpleasantnesses still weighed, to be sure, upon the atmosphere of relations. But even the fall of Khrushchev had not canceled out many of the favorable changes in Soviet conditions against which Soviet-American relations had to proceed; modest improvements and gradual ones, to be sure, but not without their significance. The terror had been mitigated. The independence of the secret police had been greatly curtailed. There had been some relaxation of the restrictions on association of Russians with foreigners. There was a greater willingness on the part of the authorities to permit many forms of participation by Soviet citizens in international life, culturally and in the sports. These changes were, to be sure, only partially recognized in Washington. Many people, as the future would show, remained quite blind to them. But LBJ and his secretary of state, Dean Rusk, were not wholly oblivious to them, nor did they fail to try to take some advantage of them. The result was that certain gains were made, in the 1966–1968 period which, if one had been able to build further on them, might well have developed into the sort of thing that later, in the early 1970s, came to be known as "détente." (The word was in fact even then in use.) Agreements were reached on the opening up of direct airline communications, on the establishment of consular representation in cities other than the respective capitals, and (in very modest measure) on certain fishing problems. New arrangements for cultural exchange were agreed upon, and the first soundings were taken for what were later to be the SALT talks and the collaboration in space exploration and research.

These beginnings soon fell victim, however, to two developments: first, the Soviet action in Czechoslovakia in 1968; secondly, and of much greater importance, the American involvement in Vietnam. It was not until the first could be forgotten, and the second brought into process of liquidation in the early 1970s, that prospects again opened up for further progress along the lines pioneered by Messrs. Johnson and Rusk some four to six years earlier.

IX

The positive results of the phase of Soviet-American relations that came to be known (somewhat misleadingly) as the Nixon-Kissinger détente are too recent to require extensive recapitulation. These results were compressed, for the most part, into an extraordinarily short period, but one full of activity: from the time of the Kissinger visit to China in the summer of 1971 to the Brezhnev visit to the United States in June 1973. The individual bilateral agreements arrived at in the course of the various negotiations and high-level visits were too numerous to be listed here. They covered some fifteen to twenty subjects, sometimes overlapping, and sometimes representing successive stages in the treatment of a single subject. Not all of them were of great political importance; a number of them represented beginnings rather than the full-fledged achievement of wholly open, fruitful, and secure arrangements; but they represented steps forward. The most important of them was, without question, the SALT agreement signed by Messrs. Nixon and Brezhnev on the occasion of the former's visit to Moscow in May 1972.

These were all bilateral Soviet-American agreements. They were flanked, of course, in their early stages, by the achievements of what came to be called Chancellor Willy Brandt's "Ostpolitik." (Again, this was a poor term—as though this were the first German government, or the last, ever to have a policy towards the East.) There were also the highly confusing and largely meaningless negotiations that were to lead, eventually, to the Helsinki agreements—multilateral negotiations in which the Americans took only an unenthusiastic and secondary part. But by and large, the Nixon-Kissinger détente was a movement of a positive nature in bilateral Soviet-American relations, observed even with some uncertainty and misgiving by America's European allies.

From the Soviet standpoint this effort of policy was stimulated and made possible by two changes in the international situation that marked the early 1970s: the liquidation of America's Vietnam involvement and the Nixon visit to Peking, followed by the establishment of a de facto American-Chinese official relationship. At the American end it was of course simultaneously the presence in positions of authority in Washington of two men: Richard Nixon, then at the height of his power and prestige, bringing to the White House a reputation as a Cold War hard-liner which gave him a certain margin of immunity from right-wing attack as he moved to improve relations with Russia; and Henry Kissinger, who brought to the operation a measure of imagination, boldness of approach, and sophistication of understanding without which it would have been difficult to achieve.

Both sides saw in this effort towards the improvement and enrichment of the relationship a chance for reducing the dangers of unlimited rivalry and proliferation in the field of nuclear weaponry; and both, be it said to their credit, were aware of the immense, almost mandatory importance of progress in this direction. In addition to this, the Soviet side saw reinforcement for itself in its relations with Communist China, and a measure of assurance against too intimate or exclusive an association between that power and the United States. The American side was astute enough to realize that the various rigidities that marked the Cold War, both as a state of mind in America and as a condition of American-Soviet relations, were not conducive to American interests in other areas of the world. In addition to this it is evident that Mr. Nixon was not wholly indifferent to the domestic-political fruits to be derived from the drama of successive summit meetings.

These recognitions, however, also roughly defined and delimited the aims and the scope of détente. Beyond them, it was not possible to go. The Soviet leaders were determined that the development should not affect the intactness of the dictatorship at home; nor was it to hinder them from continuing to adopt, with relation to the problems of third countries, a rhetorical and political stance of principled revolutionary Marxism, designed to protect them from charges by the Chinese Communists that they were betraying the cause of Marxism-Leninism. There is no evidence that they ever attempted to conceal from their Western opposite numbers the nature of the seriousness of these reservations.

Whether, in their actions affecting the 1973 Middle Eastern war and—somewhat later—Angola, the Soviet authorities did not violate at least the spirit of the earlier understandings with Messrs. Nixon and Kissinger is a question that surpasses the limits of this examination. But some people on the American side certainly thought that this was the case; and the impression was used to justify the very clear changes that did occur in American policy.

The pressures against détente had never been absent in Washington, even at the height of its development; they had only been repressed by the momentary prestige and authority of the White House. As the power of the Nixon presidency disintegrated in 1973 and 1974, the anti-détente forces moved again to the battle lines, and with great effectiveness. This was, to some extent, only to be expected; for the overdramatization of the earlier contacts and negotiations had bred false hopes and concepts of what could be achieved; and a certain disillusionment was inevitable. The signs of this reaction were already apparent in late 1973. Efforts to save the situation by another (and very misconceived) Nixon visit to Moscow, in June 1974, were unavailing. Some limited further progress was made, to be sure, in the field of cultural exchanges. But by this time, resistance in the Pentagon and elsewhere to any further concessions of consequence in the SALT talks, as well as to any acts of self-restraint in the development of American weapons programs, was too strong to be overcome, particularly by a desperate and harassed Nixon, or even by a bewildered Gerald Ford, by no means personally unresponsive to hard-line pressures.

The Jackson-Vanik Amendment, and the subsequent demise of the trade pact, dealt a bitter blow to any hopes for retaining the very considerable momentum that had been obtained in the development of Soviet-American relations. The very modest and tentative results of the Vladivostok meeting

led only to new protests and attacks from anti-détente forces
that now had the bit in their teeth and were not to be gainsaid.
By the beginning of 1975, although the various cultural agreements reached under the heading of détente were still in effect
and were being, so far as can be judged from the public reports,
punctiliously observed by both sides, the prospects for further
success in the SALT talks had been heavily damaged, and along
with them the political atmosphere in which, alone, further
progress could be made in the improvement of the Soviet-
American relationship generally.

What followed—the wrangling over the language of the
Helsinki agreements, the conflict over Angola, even the most
recent spate of expressions of alarm in Washington over the
pace of development of the Soviet armed forces—these were
in the main the products rather than the causes of the limited
deterioration of the Soviet-American relationship which the
period since mid-1973 has witnessed.

X

It would be idle to pretend, as the year 1976 runs its course,
that the prospects for the future of Soviet-American relations
are anything less than problematical. Formidable impediments
continue to lie across the path of any efforts at improvement.
The Soviet authorities will no doubt continue to adhere to
internal practices of a repressive nature that will continue to
offend large sections of American opinion. They will continue
to guard what they consider their right or their duty to subject
the United States to periodic rhetorical denunciation and to
give to anti-American political factions in third countries forms
of support that Americans will find unreconcilable with a desire
for good relations with this country. They will, rather because
they are Russians than because they are Communists, continue
to cultivate and maintain armed forces on a scale far greater
than any visible threat to their security would seem to warrant.
They will continue what they will describe as efforts to achieve
parity with the United States in naval and long-range nuclear
capabilities; and others will continue to be in doubt as to

whether these are not really efforts to achieve a decisive, and irrevocable, superiority. They will continue to hide all their undertakings behind a wholly unnecessary degree of secrecy—a secrecy which invites exaggerated fears on the other side and enhances the very dangers to which it is supposed to be responsive. None of this will be helpful to the development of the relationship.

On the other hand, the Soviet leadership has, and will continue to have, a high degree of awareness of the dangers of a continued nuclear competition. Along with all its exaggerated military efforts, it does not want, and will not want, a world war. It has a keen realization of the suicidal nature of any nuclear war; and it has too many internal problems to allow it to wish to assume inordinate risks. It is now governed, furthermore, by a relatively old, habit-worn, and weary bureaucracy, which is going to have to give over in the relatively near future. Waiting in the wings is a new generation of officials who, insofar as one is able to judge them at all, would appear to be no less tough than their elders, no less capable, and certainly no less nationalistic, but more pragmatic, less confined by ideological rigidities, less inhibited in association and converse with foreigners. To which must be added that curious streak of friendly and sometimes even admiring interest in the United States—a mixture of curiosity, eagerness for peaceful rivalry, and sometimes even real liking—that runs through the Soviet population and has never failed to be noted by observant American students of Russian life.

All these factors lend assurance that, given an American policy reasonably adjusted to these contradictions of the official Russian personality and conscious of the immensity of what is at stake in the future of the relationship, there need be no greater danger of apocalyptic disaster arising out of that relationship than there has been in the past—and the United States, after all, has contrived to live in the same world with this regime for over half a century without finding it necessary to resort to arms against it in order to protect American interests. Possibly there could even be a further successful effort to improve things.

But if this is to occur, American statesmanship will have to overcome some of the traits that have handicapped it in the past in dealing with this most unusual, most dangerous, and most serious of all the problems of foreign policy it has ever had to face. It will have to overcome that subjectivity that caused Americans to be strongly pro-Soviet at the height of the Stalin era and equally anti-Soviet in the days of Khrushchev, and to acquire a greater steadiness and realism of vision before the phenomenon of Soviet power. It will have to make greater progress than it has made to date in controlling the compulsions of the military-industrial complex and in addressing itself seriously to the diminution, whether by agreement or by unilateral restraint or both, of the scope and intensity of the weapons race.

American politicians will have to learn to resist the urge to exploit, as a target for rhetorical demonstrations of belligerent vigilance, the image of a formidable external rival in world affairs. And American diplomacy will have to overcome, in greater measure than it has done to date, those problems of privacy of decision and long-term consistency of behavior which, as Tocqueville once pointed out, were bound to burden American democracy when the country rose to the stature of a great power. In all of this, American statesmanship will need the support of a press and communications media more serious, and less inclined to oversimplify and dramatize in their coverage of American foreign policy, than what we have known in the recent past.

It is not impossible for American government and society to make these advances. To do so, they have only to match the best examples of American statesmanship in the past, but then to give to their achievements, this time, a more enduring commitment and a deeper general understanding than was the case at other high moments of American performance.

There is not, however, infinite time for the achievement of these results. Certain of the trends of international life at this moment for which the United States bears a very special responsibility, notably the steady expansion and proliferation of nuclear weaponry and the preposterous development of the export of arms from major industrial countries, are ones which it is impossible to project much farther into the future without inviting catastrophes too apocalyptic to contemplate. The greatest mistake American policymakers could make, as the country moves into the years of a new administration, would be to assume that time is not running out on all of us, themselves included.

IS DÉTENTE
WORTH
SAVING?

(1976)

Some years ago, for reasons I have never entirely understood, an impression got about that there was beginning, in our relationship with the Soviet Union, a new period of normalization and relaxation of tensions, to be sharply distinguished from all that had gone before and to be known by the term "détente."

This image of détente, in which, for all I know, there may have been at one time some slender basis of reality, came to be rather seriously oversold. It was oversold—for different reasons in each case—by our government, by the Soviet government, and by the American press; and as a result of this overselling, many people came to address to the behavior of both countries expectations that were unreal and could not be met fully.

Today an almost predictable reaction has set in—a reaction against what people understand to be "détente." It has set in partly as a consequence of the earlier overselling of this idea; partly because real mistakes have been made here and there, on both sides; partly because an improvement in political relations appeared to threaten the formidable interests vested in a continuing state of high military tension. In addition, there seem to be a number of people in our political and journalistic world for whom a certain Cold War rhetoric has long been the staff of life, who have been alarmed by an apparent favorable trend in our relationship to Russia that has threatened to undermine the basis for this rhetoric, and who now welcome the chance to attack that trend. The result has been the emergence of a school of thought which appears to believe that something useful could now be achieved in our relations with Russia by a policy of strident hostility on our part, by reversion to the Cold War slogans of the fifties, by calling names and making faces, by piling up still greater quantities of superfluous armaments, and by putting public pressure on Moscow to change its internal practices, and indeed the very nature of Soviet power.

Granted this tangle of motivations and outlooks, just where should the United States stand regarding détente? Is it a mere governmental public-relations ploy, without grounding in the realities? Or is it a major fact of international life, which will lead on to ever-widening vistas of mutual Soviet-American support?

The best way of getting at these questions is, it seems to me, to step back from them so that the riddle of détente can be brought into historical perspective.

There is no need to dwell at any great length on the curious sort of symmetry—sometimes one of similarity, sometimes of diametrical opposition—that has marked the development of the Russian and American peoples, particularly in the modern age—by which term I am thinking of the past 200 to 250 years. Many thoughtful observers—including even Tocqueville, who had never been to Russia—have noted it and commented on it. At the start of that period, the two peoples were marked by their respective inhabitation of vast, underpopulated, and relatively underdeveloped but potentially enormously fruitful territories in the North Temperate Zone of the planet. In the eighteenth century both were just emerging out of a former obscurity onto the great stage of the international life of the civilized world. The Russians were emerging into this limelight after several centuries of relative isolation—which one might call a historically compelled isolation—from the main cultural and religious and political centers of Western civilization. They were emerging in the manner with which we are all

familiar. By that time a limited westward territorial expansion
had brought them to Poland and to the Baltic Sea. The construction of a new and partially Europeanized capital on the
banks of the Neva was creating a governmental center reasonably open to contact with Western Europe, in contrast to the
former remote and self-immolating Grand Duchy of Muscovy,
with its religious intolerance, its dark suspicion of the heretical
outside world, its pious abhorrence of contact with the individual Western foreigner.

In that same century we Americans were emerging onto the
world scene for the first time as a discrete entity, but emerging
in quite a different way: not as an old people, isolated from
Europe by the workings of a long and unhappy history, but as
a young people newly born, so to speak, out of the wombs of
old England and Scotland and certain parts of the Continent.
We bore with us, to be sure, the traditions, the customs, the
inherited outlooks of the European societies that had mothered
us. But we were now in the process of being changed to some
degree by the very discipline of our physical encounter with the
great American wilderness and were, in any case, appearing
now for the first time as something in our own right, something
visible and active on the landscape of world politics, preparing
to take an independent part in the affairs of the world.

To this concept we must add, now, the reflection that
around the same time both of these two peoples, starting from
a position of what we might call proximity to the main centers
of Western European power and culture, began in earnest their
respective processes of developmental expansion away from
those centers: the Russians eastward across the Volga and the
Urals into the immense expanses of Central Asia and Siberia;
the Americans westward across their own empty, magnificent,
and underdeveloped continent. Both were destined, in the late
nineteenth and early twentieth centuries, to close the circle
and to meet, in a sense, on the shores of the Pacific—to meet
as peoples by this time of immense demographic, physical, and
potential military power, each towering already in these respects over any of the individual entities, if not the totality, of
the old Europe from which they had taken, in so high degree,
their origins and their inspirations.

So far I have dealt mostly with similarities. But these similarities in physical and geographic experience were accompanied by profound, almost antithetically related differences in political and social outlook. With these differences, too, most of us are familiar. The Russians inherited the outlook of a great continental land power, almost totally cut off from the world oceans, surrounded over great periods of their history by fierce and dangerous land neighbors; and they became accustomed to that intense concentration of political authority that marks all societies and communities that find themselves virtually in a state of siege. The Russians learned to regard as natural the subordination of the individual to this concentration of authority. They were grateful, no doubt, for whatever liberties and immunities might be conceded to the individual at any given moment, but they tended to accept these as the product of an act of grace on the part of constituted authority rather than as absolute rights, inherent in the condition of individual man. We Americans, on the other hand, were heirs to the mercantile and commercial traditions of latter-day England and Scotland. Shielded in effect on the oceanic side—whether we recognized the fact or not—by English sea power, and facing on our mainland only insignificant military challenges, we were able to proceed in relative peace to the development of our continent, enjoying, indeed taking increasingly for granted, these rights and procedures of self-government that were actually in high degree the achievements of the European civilizations out of which we had emerged.

The differences between these two outlooks were, as you see, profound. But the two peoples had one thing in common: a tendency to attribute to their own political ideology a potential universal validity—to perceive in it virtues that ought, as one thought, to command not only imitation on the part of other peoples everywhere but also recognition of the moral authority and ascendancy of the respective national center from which these virtues were proceeding. The Russians had inherited this messianic view of their own place in the world from old Byzantium, with its strong sense of religious orthodoxy and its universalistic political pretensions. We Americans had it because, failing to recognize the relationship between our freedoms and

achievements on the one hand, and the uniquely favorable
conditions in which it was given to us to lead our national life
on the other, we mistook those achievements and freedoms as
the products of some peculiar wisdom and virtue on our own
part and came to see in the system of government we were now
enjoying the ultimate salvation of most of the rest of the world.
So each of these great peoples went along into the twentieth
century nurturing vague dreams, if not of world power, at least
of a species of exemplary and moral world leadership, which
entitled it to some special form of admiration, deference, imitation, or authority—call it what you will—at the hands of other
less favorably endowed peoples.

It was, then, against this background that the relations between the two peoples and their governments developed up to
the end of the nineteenth century. In the geopolitical sense
there were no serious conflicts between them; on the contrary,
there was much, particularly in their respective relationships to
England, that gave to each of them a certain limited positive
value in the other's eyes. But ideologically the two official
establishments remained poles apart. They viewed each other
with uneasiness and distaste. The image of tsarist autocracy
remained no less repulsive in American eyes than did American
republicanism in the eyes of the court and bureaucracy of
Petersburg. And over the whole period of tsarist power these
differences continued to constitute a complicating factor in
Russian-American relations, not wholly inhibiting the development of those relations but limiting in some degree the dimensions and intensity they could assume.

Toward the end of the nineteenth century, another complication began to make itself felt in the form of the growing
restlessness of the non-Russian nationalities within the framework of the Russian Empire and the growing power of their
appeals to congressional and, to some extent, popular sympathies within this country. This was a factor that has to be
distinguished from the general incompatibility of the two political systems to which I have just referred, because this restlessness arose not mainly from discontent with the general political
system prevailing in Russia (although there was this, too), but

rather from the treatment by the tsarist regime of the particular non-Russian nationality in question, which was a different thing. The phenomenon became a complicating factor in Russian-American relations only when individuals from among these minority nationalities began to appear in significant numbers among the immigrants to this country. Particularly was this true, of course, of the Jews—Russian, Polish, and Lithuanian—whose migration to this country in considerable numbers began in earnest in the 1880s, and whose powerful resentment of the treatment of their co-religionists in Russia soon began to be a factor of importance in American political life. The legislative branch of the American government has always had, it would seem, a peculiar sensitivity to the feeling of compact blocks of recent immigrants residing in our great urban communities. So, at any rate, it was in this case, with the result that the tales of the sufferings of these non-Russian nationalities soon came to exercise upon political and congressional opinion in this country an influence stronger than anything ever evoked by the tales of the sufferings of the Russian people themselves at the hands of their autocratic government. It is curious, in a certain melancholy way, to recall that in December 1911 the House of Representatives adopted almost unanimously a resolution calling on the president to terminate the old trade treaty with Russia that had been in force ever since 1832; and the purpose of this resolution was to compel the Russian government to liberalize its treatment of the Jews within Russia. The one vote cast against the resolution in the House of Representatives was cast by a man who complained that this sort of pressure by a foreign government would not help the Jews in Russia but would appreciably damage American business; President Taft, pursuant to this resolution, did so terminate the treaty, with the result that Russian-American relations, down to the Revolution of 1917, remained very cool and unhappy indeed.

This, then, was the general shape of Russian-American relations as they existed in the final years of the tsarist empire, and it was against this background that the whole question was overtaken by the Russian Revolution, in 1917.

The initial impact of this revolution on the relationship consisted primarily of sheer confusion. The reaction of the American public was confused by the fact that it was not one revolution but two: a moderate-democratic one in February 1917, with which all Americans tended to sympathize; and an extreme, left-wing-Marxist one, dictatorially oriented, in November, the seriousness and durability of which was at first widely questioned. This reaction was even more confused by the fact that there was at that time a war in progress—a great European war which the United States was then just in the process of entering. The emotional reaction to the experience of being at war soon came to dominate American opinion and to distort all other issues. Thus the Russian Provisional Government, resulting from the first revolution, was idealized because it attempted to carry on in the war against Germany, whereas the Bolshevik regime, taking over in November 1917, was scorned, resented, and opposed in large measure because its first official act was to take Russia out of the war entirely.

Similar confusions prevailed, of course, on the Bolshevik side. Lenin and his associates attached enormous significance to their own seizure of power. They saw it as the first step in a political transformation of the world far more important than any of the issues over which the world war was being fought. And for this reason they insisted on seeing America's reluctant and trivial participation in the Allied military intervention in Russia, in 1918–1920, as the expression of an ideological hostility to themselves, rather than as an event in the prosecution of the war against Germany, which it really was.

These early confusions and misunderstandings yielded only slowly and partially to the passage of time, and they helped to engender a deep mutual antagonism between the two parties concerned. But they were not the most important cause of the antagonism. The most important cause was another situation produced by the Revolution—a situation that was not at all a misunderstanding: the fact, namely, that the Bolshevik leaders looked upon the political and social system of this country as a misconceived, regressive, iniquitous one, disreputable in its origins and purposes and deserving of violent overthrow; and they conceived it as their duty, however poor the prospects for success, to encourage such an overthrow and to contribute to its realization wherever they could. This too, of course, bred a reciprocal reaction here. It was a reaction flowing in part from resentment of the Soviet attitude—resentment, that is, of the hostility addressed by the Bolshevik leaders to cherished American ideals and institutions. But it also flowed from a very genuine distaste on the part of most Americans for what they could learn of the ideology of the new Communist leaders and of the manner in which their dictatorial authority was being exercised.

So the Russian-American relationship came to be burdened in the twenties and thirties not only by the great differences in historical experience and political tradition of which I have spoken but also by those special elements of ideological and political antagonism introduced by the establishment of Communist power in Russia.

All of this was sufficient to render relations in the period between the two wars—not just in the early years of nonrecognition but even after diplomatic relations were established in 1933—distant, meager, and unpleasant. Now these sources of contention were in their entirety a serious burden on an international relationship (and no one could have been more aware of their seriousness, I think, than those of us who served in the American Embassy in Moscow at the time). But they were not, I would point out, the source of any particular military tension between the two countries; and there was no great urgency about the resolution of the conflicts they produced. They represented serious long-term problems, but these were not problems wholly immune to those immutable laws of change that eventually affect all societies, transform all customs, and erode all militant ideologies; and for this reason there was no need to despair of their ultimate peaceful resolution. Above all, the preservation of world peace, not to mention the inviolability of civilized life on the planet, did not depend on their early solution.

It was in this last respect, above all, that the outcome of World War II worked its most significant and most fateful changes. There are two of these changes that stand out in my mind. Both were of a quasi-military nature.

The first was the elimination of Germany and Japan as major military powers standing between the United States and the Soviet Union, the attendant creation of great political and military vacuums, and the advance of Soviet military power, by way of filling one of these vacuums, into the heart of Europe. This produced a direct confrontation between American and Soviet military power that had never existed before.

As far as conventional forces were concerned, even this was not necessarily a fatal complication. The presence of both Soviet and American forces in the heart of Europe is an anomaly of history, awkward in some ways to both parties and to the peoples whose territory is affected. For this very reason, given continuing restraint and patience on both sides, it may be expected to yield eventually to a more normal and less dangerous state of affairs.

The same, unfortunately, cannot be said of the second of the two great military-political consequences of World War II, for this was the acquisition and cultivation by both American and Soviet governments of the nuclear capability—of the capability, that is, of putting an end to civilized life not only on the territory of the other party but on great portions of the remainder of the surface of the planet as well.

The fears and other reactions engendered by this nuclear rivalry have now become a factor in our relations with Russia of far greater actual importance than the underlying ideological and political differences. The real conflicts of interest and outlook, for all their seriousness, are limited ones. There is nothing in them that could not yield to patience, change, and a readiness for accommodation. There is nothing in them, above all, that could really be solved by—and, therefore, nothing that could justify—a major war, let alone the sort of global cataclysm that seems to pre-empt so many of our plans and discussions. Yet this fact is constantly being crowded out of our consciousness by the prominence, and the misleading implications, of the military competition. An image arises, if only initially for purposes of military planning, of an utterly inhuman adversary, committed to our total destruction, and committed to it not for any coherent political reason but only because he has the capacity to inflict it. This unreal image presents itself to both parties; and in the name of a response to it whole great economies are distorted, whole populations are to some extent impoverished, vast amounts of productive capacity needed for constructive purposes in a troubled world are devoted to sterile and destructive ones; a proliferation of nuclear weaponry is encouraged and pursued that only increases with every day the dimensions and dangers of the problem to which it is supposed to be responsive; and the true nature of our relations with the Soviet Union and its peoples becomes obscured and distorted by the cloud of anxieties and panicky assumptions that falls across its face. The nuclear rivalry, in other words, begins to ride along of its own momentum, like an object in space, divorced from any cause or rationale other than the fears it engenders, corrupting and distorting a relationship that, while not devoid of serious problems, never needed to be one of mortal antagonism.

Our first task, then, is to master, and to bring under rational control, this fearful capacity for suicidal destruction that has been let loose among us; and of this I would say only that so terrible are the dangers of a continued failure to master it that we would be fully warranted in accepting very considerable risks to avoid this failure. The risks, for example, of a total ban on the testing of nuclear weapons seem to me to be trivial in comparison with the risks involved in the continued proliferation of these weapons on a world scale. Yet we shrink from it. Is this timidity really justified? Is the tail of military fear not wagging the dog of constructive and hopeful political opportunity at this point?

I find myself disturbed by these reactions not only because of their obvious negativeness and sterility, and not only because they stimulate exaggerations and distortions of the real situation in world affairs, but also because they tend to obscure both the real limitations and the real possibilities to which our relations with the Soviet Union are subject. Let us remember that for the reasons I have just outlined, there has always been an

area where collaboration with Russia, as we would like to see
it, has not been possible. This was true before the Revolution.
It is true today. It will continue to be true long into the future.
But there is another area in which collaboration—and mutually
profitable collaboration—*is* possible. The relative size and nature of these two areas is not immutable; it has not failed to
change with the years; and only someone unfamiliar with the
history of Soviet-American relations could fail to recognize that
since Stalin's death the direction of this change has been in
general a favorable one—the one we would like to see.

This has been, if you will, a small gain, but it has been a real
one and the only kind we can hope to make. And it should be
recognized that none of the complicating factors—neither the
asperities of our military rivalry, nor the apparent conflict of
our aims with those of the Soviet Union in specific geographic
area and countries, nor the somewhat dated but now traditional Communist rhetoric to which the Soviet leadership is
committed—none of these things constitutes any adequate
reason, nor do all of them together, why we should not exploit
to the full those areas in which our relations with Russia are
or might be capable of constructive development and where
exchanges might be pursued, cultural as well as commercial,
which would be mutually profitable and would give greater
depth and stability to the relationship as a whole.

We have burdens enough in Soviet-American relations
without adding to them by the neglect of those areas where
possibilities for improvement do actually exist. In a world so
troubled as ours of today, the favorable opportunities have to
be cherished and nurtured, not sacrificed to prejudice, vanity,
or political ambition.

4

SELECTIONS FROM INTERVIEWS

"Containment" and the Fear of a Russian Attack
(1975)

KENNAN: What I thought was essential in 1945, in 1946, and in 1947 was to prevent the political influence and predominant authority of the Soviet government from spreading any further in the world, because we had had it demonstrated in the period of World War II that you didn't always have to occupy another country in order to dominate its life. You could threaten it, or you could subvert its government by various ways, including the time-honored phenomenon of puppet government. I was afraid, I must say, at that time (and I think with some reason) of what is today called the "domino theory." Western Europe, as the war ended, was in a sorry state. People were disoriented, discouraged, apprehensive, frightened by the experiences of the war, and it would not have been too difficult for Italy or for France, if they had lost their confidence in us then, to turn to the Soviet Union and let their Communist parties take over. It seemed to me that it was important for Europe, for us, and in the long run, even for the Russians— that this should not happen. It just wasn't desirable.

When I talked about containment, what I had in mind was an effort on our part to stiffen the hope, the confidence, of European nations in themselves, and to persuade them that

they didn't need to yield to one great power or another, that
they could resume life. We would help them to do it. That was
all that was involved. I didn't think the Russians wanted to
attack anyone. I didn't think they wanted to expand any further by force of arms. I'm sure I was absolutely right about this.
In 1948, when the talk of the formation of the NATO pact
began (it was actually the Europeans—the French and the
British and the Benelux people—who came to us and wanted
it) I was quite surprised. I said, "Why are you giving your
attention to this? We're just getting the Marshall Plan
through. For goodness sake, concentrate on your economic
recovery. Nobody's going to attack you." But I found that all
of Western Europe had what the French call *la manie d'invasion*—the mania of invasion.

SEVAREID: That's what revisionists forget. It was the Europeans who were terrified to death at this period.

KENNAN: That's correct.

SEVAREID: They're less terrified than we are today, but at
that time it was quite the reverse. But are you saying, in effect,
that you didn't think NATO was really necessary then? The
other theory was that unless you had a military shield this
economic development wouldn't go forward in peace.

KENNAN: Within the course of time the military shield
probably would have had to be built, although it never had to
assume the dimensions that it has today. I think one could have
dealt with the Russians about these things. At any rate, it
should never have been given the emphasis it was given. We
should never have allowed the thesis to become established
that, if it were not for the so-called deterrent quality of our
nuclear weapons, the Russians would immediately have at-
tacked Western Europe and overrun it. I never thought this
was true.

Could the Russians Successfully
Dominate Western Europe?
(1976)

I don't think the Russians are that great—I don't think they
could do it technically. To dominate large areas with massive
populations, in the first place military occupation would be

necessary. I don't think they would relish the prospect. They would, for one thing, have a grave problem with their own troops: their exposure to the influences of a much more advanced and wealthier civilization would be certain to have a devastating effect on them. We saw this happen even during World War II when Western Europe, in the shape of Germany, offered a much less damaging standard for comparison than Western Europe would offer today.

I don't attribute to the Russians the political and ideological capability of controlling hundreds of millions of Western Europeans. They would find Western Europeans, by virtue of their numbers, background, and sophistication, much harder to regiment and control than they did the people of Eastern Europe. They have much more to put up in opposition to Soviet power. Moreover, there are limits to every form of imperialism; even the power of a militant regime-on-the-make is not unlimited. You have said that "overextension" has seldom acted as a deterrent. But I would remind you that there is such a thing as spreading oneself too thin: Napoleon showed this, and Hitler showed it too. I was stationed, as a diplomat, in Germany during part of the war, and I visited almost every Nazi-occupied country. I came away with the impression that even if Hitler had won the war, he would not have been able to maintain the empire he was trying to establish.

On the other hand, the Germans themselves had much more effective people, more capable administrators, and greater self-confidence than the Russians had ever had. When they overran a country, they had the men who spoke the language, could take charge of the railroads and the telephone system, and were not only competent to perform a great many other tasks, but were also endowed with enough self-confidence to win, to some extent, the respect of the local people. The Russians would not be able to do any of these things.

Do you think sophisticated Western Marxists would really accept Russian tutelage? Look at Moscow—it is ideologically the most bankrupt capital in the world. Its entire message is absurdly out of date—which is also the main reason for the growing restlessness of the Russian intelligentsia. The Soviet version of socialism is so absolutely stultified—it hasn't changed since 1910—that it makes no sense at all in relation to our present problems.

Of course, you *can* get a hammer lock on society through a determined minority. But, all in all, I attribute much more importance to national differences than you do. The Eastern European example is somewhat deceiving. It is true that the first generation of Eastern European leaders was selected by Moscow; but as a new generation comes along, the differences, and the spirit of independence, tend to assert themselves. I would remind you that all through Eastern Europe the intellectual acceptance of Russia is virtually nil. The Eastern Europeans regard the Russians, at best, as insufferable bores. They mock their dogmatism and the sterility of their thinking. They are certainly not under Russian cultural influence. I can see all this encapsulated in Eastern European attitudes to my own field, Russian studies, which are incomparably stronger in the United States than they are anywhere in Eastern Europe, where even the teaching of the Russian language is resisted. What I'm trying to say is that even under full Soviet hegemony the national peculiarities of individual countries would have a way of coming out on top.

"Liberation" as an Objective of American Policy
(1976)

I have, of course, no sympathy with the principles of Soviet government. I don't want to see Soviet rule preserved because I think it is admirable; but I have (and we spoke of this a little earlier) the greatest misgivings about any of us, Americans or Western Europeans, taking upon ourselves the responsibility for trying to overthrow this, or any other, government in Russia, because we have in our pockets no alternatives.

Never forget that some years before the Russian Revolution, in 1911 to be precise, we were faced with almost exactly the same problem—the persecution of Russian Jews—and we abrogated (under President Taft) a trade agreement with

Russia in protest against the treatment of Russian Jews. And my namesake, George Kennan the elder, was busy for many years trying to whip up sympathy for the Russian revolutionaries, admittedly not the Bolsheviks but their moderate predecessors, the Populists. The assumption behind all this was that if one could only overthrow the old tsarist autocracy, something much better would follow. Have we learned anything from this lesson?

I don't want to see our economic muscle applied in order to bring about the destruction of Soviet power. I don't want to have any responsibility at all for what happens in Russian affairs for, as I have just said, I am not at all sure that what would come after it would be any better than what we have today. I can see no evidence in Russia of any understanding of the principles of democracy, except on the part of Sakharov and a very small number of dissidents.

As a matter of fact, Russia was much more fit for democratic development in 1914 than she is today. Mind you, she was not very fit *then*, but she was better equipped than she is in 1976 because, in the meantime, some fifty million people have died unnatural deaths in the Soviet Union, among them a very high percentage of the more thoughtful, cultured, and sensitive people who alone would have been able to guide Russian political life in a more liberal direction. Today you will find that many of the people who, for one reason or another, run away from Russia in opposition to the Soviet government and end up on our shores aren't at all looking for a liberal-democratic alternative—that while they may be anti-Soviet, their ideals of how Russia ought to be governed are heavily affected by their experiences of living in a totalitarian society. The Soviet regime has rubbed off on them.

I am very skeptical about the limits of their tolerance. These people are very Russian, and the idea of compromise, especially in the ideological field, is alien to them. And it is as well to remember that this has always been the way with the Russians. If you follow the development of Russian political life between 1906 and 1914, the striking thing is the gross intolerance that existed, not just on the side of the government, but in the whole of Russian society. Indeed it is true to say that, from the Decembrists to the Bolshevik Revolution, the intolerance, the unwillingness to compromise, to permit gradual improvement, was greater within the revolutionary movement than it was on the part of the autocracy.

Two Views of Soviet Leadership
(1978)

There are basically two views of leadership: two ways in which it is seen in this country.

In one of these views, the Soviet leaders appear as a terrible and forbidding group of men: monsters of sorts, really, because lacking in all elements of common humanity—men totally dedicated either to the destruction or to the political undoing and enslavement of this country and its allies—men who have all internal problems, whether of civic obedience or of economic development, essentially solved and are therefore free to spend their time evolving elaborate schemes for some ultimate military showdown—men who are prepared to accept the most tremendous risks, and to place upon their people the most fearful sacrifices, if only in this way their program of destruction or domination of ourselves and our allies can be successfully carried forward.

That is one view. In the other view, these leaders are seen as a group of quite ordinary men, to some extent the victims, if you will, of the ideology on which they have been reared, but shaped far more importantly by the discipline of the responsibilities they and their predecessors have borne as rulers of a great country in the modern technological age. They are seen, in this view, as highly conservative men, perhaps the most conservative ruling group to be found anywhere in the world, markedly advanced in age, approaching the end of their tenure, and given to everything else but rash adventure. They are seen as men who share the horror of major war that dominates most of the Soviet people, who have no desire to experience another military conflagration and no intention to launch one—men more seriously concerned to preserve the present limits of their political power and responsibility than to expand those limits

—men whose motivation is essentially defensive and whose attention is riveted primarily to the unsolved problems of economic development within their own country. They are seen as men who suffer greatly under the financial burden which the maintenance of the present bloated arsenals imposes on the Soviet economy, and who would like to be relieved of that burden if this could be accomplished without undue damage to Russia's security and to their own political prestige. They are seen, finally, as men who are, to be sure, seldom easy to deal with, who care more about appearances than about reality, who have an unfortunate fixation about secrecy which complicates their external relations in many ways, but who, despite all these handicaps, have good and sound reason, rooted in their own interests, for desiring a peaceful and constructive relationship with the United States within the area where that is theoretically possible.

I would submit that it is these two conflicting views of the Soviet leadership that lie at the heart of the conflict between those in our government who are attempting to make progress in our relations with the Soviet Union and those who are attacking this effort from the right. And the burden of what I have to say is that I think we can no longer permit this great conflict of outlook and opinion to go on in so large degree unreconciled as it has gone in recent years—that the moment has come when we can no longer carry on safely or effectively in our relations with the Soviet Union without the creation of a much wider consensus of opinion behind our policies of the moment than anything we have known in this recent period.

Détente and Its Opponents
(1978)

I

Détente has been oversold in America so that the United States public does not understand how the Russians interpret the concept and how we should react to that interpretation.

We should have recognized from the very start that there is only a narrow area in which profitable collaboration is possible between ourselves and the Soviet government. There is a large area in which it is not possible.

Nevertheless, I would not be trying to set up an Institute for Advanced Russian Studies [at the Smithsonian Institution] if I thought that there weren't areas for productive exchange with the Soviet Union. When I look back over the years—and my memories go back farther than almost anybody's who speaks on this subject—I see a certain improvement in the sense that the area of collaboration is broader today than it was in the Stalin period. It is a slow improvement, but it is not insignificant; and I see no reason for throwing the baby out with the bath water and returning to the Cold War policy of name-calling, hurling threats at each other, and hounding our own people because they are suspected of having had some sympathy with the Soviet Union many years ago.

I don't want to go back to all that, and I cannot for the life of me understand what it is that our hard-liners in this country really want. They want more armaments, of course, nothing like this pittance of a hundred billion dollars for defense. The defense budget, they demand, should be much larger than that and, with it, the national budgetary deficit and our inflation. But suppose they get a much larger defense budget; suppose we arm to the teeth; suppose that instead of having 15,000–20,000 nuclear weapons, we make ourselves happy by having 35,000. The fact of the matter is that 200 would make life impossible anywhere we wanted to.

But suppose we found some comfort in these vast figures, suppose we achieved a much stronger stance, and then sat back and hurled imprecations at the Soviet leaders and their system —where would we go from there? I don't see much future in this; I can't see how anyone would benefit. I suppose some naïve people would then want us to say, "Now we are very strong—we have 35,000 of these weapons, you have only 28,-000; we will put our terms to you, and you do what we want you to do, or else." I don't think this would work—blackmail can act both ways.

I notice there has been some talk of demanding political concessions from the Russians as a *quid pro quo* for United States wheat. This, too, would be a very unwise course to enter upon.

II

The effort to pursue a balanced and useful middle course in the relationship with Russia has never been an easy one for American policymakers to follow; and one of the main reasons why this has been so difficult is that seldom, if ever, have we had an adequate consensus in American opinion on the nature of the problem and the most promising ways of approaching it.

Prior to the late 1940s—prior, that is, to the Korean War and the death of Stalin—the difficulty seemed to come primarily from the left: from people who had a naïve, overtrusting, overidealistic view of what was then Stalinist power—people who thought it really possible for this country to ingratiate itself with the Stalin regime by various one-sided gestures of confidence and generosity and reproached our government for not doing so. It was, incidentally, against this sort of left-wing deviation that my X article—and the policy of containment— was directed.

But since Stalin's death, the opposition to an even-handed and realistic policy towards Russia has tended to come from the opposite end of the political spectrum: from people who were unable to see the curious mix of the negative and the positive, of the discouraging and the hopeful, in the Soviet political personality—people who could see only the negative, and who feared the consequences of anything less than a total rejection and hostility from our side. There has never been a time in these last twenty-five years, it seems to me, when this opposition has not made itself felt. There has never been a time when American statesmen concerned to find and develop a construc-

tive middle ground in relations with Russia have not felt their
efforts harassed from that direction.

III

In the heyday of the Nixon-Kissinger *détente,* this opposition was almost silenced, partly by Richard Nixon's formidable
credentials as a hard-liner, which bewildered many critics, and
partly by Henry Kissinger's diplomatic fireworks, which daz-
zled them. But the resulting silence was one of frustration, not
of acceptance. When Watergate drained the authority of this
political combination, the opposition broke forth once again
with redoubled strength and violence.

It has raged over the entire period from 1975 to the present.
It sufficed to knock out the 1974 trade agreement and to lower
the level of Soviet-American trade. It sufficed to delay the
approach to a new SALT agreement. And it has achieved
today, against the background of a new administration and a
somewhat unstructured Congress, a power it never had before.
It now claims to have—and for all I know it does have—the
power to veto any Soviet-American agreements in the military
or the economic field that do not meet with its requirements;
and such are its requirements that I come increasingly to suspect that this means, in effect, any conceivable agreements
at all.

I have made my best efforts to understand the rationale of
this opposition. Many of the bearers of it are my friends. I
know them as honorable people. I do not suspect, or disrespect,
their motives.

It is clear that we have to do here with a complex phenomenon, not a simple one. This body of opinion embraces some
people whose trouble seems to be that they are unaware of the
changes between 1947 and 1977, who talk of the problems of
Soviet-American relations in terms identical with those used at
the height of the Cold War—who sometimes seem, in fact,
unaware that Stalin is dead.

Then there are others whose emotions have been aroused
over the question of human rights, or of Jewish emigration, and

who would like to see American policy directed, not to an accommodation to Soviet power as it is, but to the changing of the very nature of the Soviet regime.

More important, however, than either of these are the people who view the relationship exclusively as one of military rivalry, who see in it no significant values or issues or possibilities other than ones relating to the supposed determination of the Soviet leadership to achieve some sort of decisive military ascendancy over the NATO coalition—and this, of course, with the most menacing and deadly of intent. These include outstandingly the military planners, whose professional obligation it is to set up a planner's dummy of any possible military opponent, to endow that dummy with just the motivation I have described, and then to treat it as if it were real. But this group also includes many nonmilitary people who, accepting this dummy as the reality, lose themselves in the fantastic reaches of what I might call military mathematics—the mathematics of possible mutual destruction in an age of explosively burgeoning weapons technology.

I have made my efforts to understand the arguments of these military enthusiasts. I have tried to follow them through the mazes of their intricate and sophisticated calculations of possible military advantage at various future points in time. I have tried to follow them in their recital of the letters and numbers of various weapons systems, some real, some imagined; their comparisons of the reputed capacities of these systems; their computations of the interactions of them in situations of actual hostility.

I come away from this exercise frustrated, and with two overpowering impressions. The first is that this entire science of long-range massive destruction—of calculated advantage or disadvantage in modern weaponry—has gotten seriously out of hand; that the variables, the complexities, the uncertainties it involves are rapidly growing beyond the power of either human mind or computer.

But my second impression is that there is a distinct unreality about this whole science of destruction—unreality, that is, when you view it as the plane on which our differences over policy have to be resolved. I doubt that we are going to solve our problems by trying to agree as to whether the Russians will or will not have the capability of "taking out" our land-based missiles at some time in the 1980s. I doubt that this is the heart of the problem. I suspect that something deeper is here involved. And if I had to try to define that deeper something, I would have to say that it is the view one takes of the nature of the Soviet leadership and of the discipline exerted upon it by its own experiences, problems, and political necessities.

The Helsinki Agreements
(1976)

Helsinki was a sterile two-year exercise in semantics which was bound to lead to very little. I have always said that I did not believe in trying to reach agreements with the Russians on general principles. The first advice given by the first representative in Russia of the London Muscovy Company under Queen Elizabeth I was: "When you deal with these people, make your bargains plain and put them in writing." This still holds true today. I believe in dealing with the Soviet government on specifics. I would not sign any agreement with them which went beyond stating: "This is what *you* undertake to do, and this is what *we* undertake to do." The idea of saying that we are both going to behave like good democrats, that we are both going to recognize human rights and so forth, is a mistake from the beginning.

Finlandization and Nuclear Blackmail
(1976)

The Finns have put certain restraints on themselves in matters which they felt would give serious offense on the other side of the border. But Finland is a small country of four million people which has a long and extremely exposed border with the Soviet Union and lies very close to Russia's second city. I cannot see how that can be compared to the position of Western Europe. I have said earlier, but let me repeat it, that Western Europe has a larger and infinitely more sophisticated as well as industrially more advanced population than the Soviet Union. Its industrial potential is much greater than that of the Soviet Union, and it is separated from the Soviet Union by a band of buffer states. Clearly, the analogy with Finland is totally inapplicable.

Now this brings me back to a point where my own thinking parts company with that of the whole of the Western European community, namely the question of nuclear blackmail and political-military pressure.

Stalin said the nuclear weapon is something with which you frighten people with weak nerves. He could not have been more right. No one in his right senses would yield to any such thing as nuclear blackmail. In the first place, it would be most unlikely (as is the case with most forms of blackmail) that the threat would be made good if one defied it. Secondly, there would be no point in yielding to it. Any regime that has not taken leave of its senses would reject the nuclear threat. "Why in the world should we give in to this?" it would argue. "If we do what you want us to do today in the name of this threat what are you going to ask us to do tomorrow? There is no end to this process. If what you want us to do is to part with our independence, you will have to find others to do your work for you, and that means that you will have to take ultimate responsibility for running this country. We are not going to be the people to turn this government into an instrument of your power."

We had experience of this kind of situation during the war with the question of the Azores. I was myself deeply involved in it, and it was quite clear that if we came along and threatened Salazar (as we almost did) and said, "You give us these bases or else we will take them," he would have picked up his hat and said, "If I have brought my country to a pass where I have to deal under this type of pressure, I am obviously not a fit ruler of this country. You will have to find someone else for it."

No one would give in to this kind of pressure; nor does anybody use this kind of blackmail. Great governments do not behave that way. Of course, Hitler did with Hacha, in the case of Czechoslovakia; but Hitler was an exception, and I am not sure that Hacha and the Czechs were wise to yield to this anyway.

Why Nuclear Weapons Should Be Totally Eliminated
(1976)

I have no high opinion of human beings: they are always going to fight and do nasty things to each other. They are always going to be part animal, governed by their emotions and subconscious drives rather than by reason. They will always, as Freud remarked, feel a grave *Unbehagen,* a discomfort, at having to live in a civilized framework, and kick against it. But if that is so, the only thing you can do with them is to see that the weapons they have are not too terrible. You must prevent them from playing with the worst kind of toys. This is why I feel that the great weapons of mass destruction—and nuclear arms are not the only conceivable ones—should never be in human hands, that it would be much better to go back, symbolically speaking, to bows and arrows, which at least do not destroy nature. I have no sympathy with the man who demands an eye for an eye in a nuclear conflict.

I would be much happier for my children (and this is, again, one of those overstatements which I must ask you not to take too literally, for I could argue against it) if we had no nuclear weapons at all—if we were in the position of Norway, which has no nuclear arms, or in the position of Mexico. The Norwegians and Mexicans have a chance. Bear in mind that if there is an incentive for the Soviet government, or any other nuclear power to use these weapons against us, it must be sought in the fact that we are ourselves developing them; only fear could lead anybody to do anything so monstrous.

The Soviet Dangers versus Ecological Disaster
(1976)

We are faced with two conceivable versions of catastrophe. One is a possible, but by no means certain, catastrophe in case we should militarily clash with the Russians. The other is an absolutely certain ecological and demographic disaster which is going to overtake this planet within the next, I would say, sixty to seventy years, but the effects of which will probably make themselves very painfully felt before the end of this century. The second of these two, if allowed to develop, may be final; there can be no real recovery from it. It is possible that some parts of humanity may survive it; but this would, at best, mean the beginning of a new Dark Age. All we have achieved in Western civilization over the last two thousand years would be lost.

In the face of this crisis, which is predictable and now almost inevitable, how can we be so absorbed with the one that is not inevitable—that is to say, the nuclear conflict with Russia—that we concentrate all our energies on the latter? Compared to the dangers which confront us on the ecological and demographic front, the possibility of Soviet control of Western Europe, even if one thought that this was a likely thing to happen (which I don't) would strike me as a minor catastrophe. After all, people *do live* in the Soviet Union. For the mass of people there, life is not intolerable. The same is true in East Germany; the same is true in Hungary. It is not what these people would like; but still, it is a way of living, and it does not mean the end of the experiment of human civilization; it leaves the way open for further developments. But from the ecological catastrophe that looms in front of us there is no recovery.

We have been putting the emphasis in the wrong places. We talk of saving Western civilization when we talk of a military confrontation with Russia—but saving it for what? In order that twenty or thirty years hence we may run out of oil, and minerals, and food, and invite upon humanity a devastating conflict between the overpopulated and undernourished two-thirds of the world and ourselves?

The differences exist and they are important. The decline of the West is not a fully accomplished fact, nor is our stumbling into this great physical catastrophe final. If we in the West could get over this fixation we have with the idea that the Russians are dying to drop bombs on us, and think, instead, of what is happening to our planet, and address ourselves, resolutely and rapidly, to preventing the catastrophe that looms before us, we would be doing a great deal better. You must remember that as far as the pollution of the earth is concerned, this is largely the work of the great industrial nations which are spread out around the fertile zones of the Northern Hemisphere. If they could be induced to behave differently, we would have a breathing space. Otherwise we are going to face irrevocable disaster. Aren't we, then (to repeat something that can never be repeated often enough), being unrealistic in the amount of attention we devote to protecting ourselves from the Russians who, God knows, are not ten feet tall, who have all sorts of troubles of their own, who can't run an agricultural system that really works, who can't adequately house their population, who are rapidly losing their prestige and leadership in the world Communist movement, and have to reckon with China on their long frontier in the East? Isn't it grotesque to spend so much of our energy on opposing such a Russia in order to save a West which is honeycombed with bewilderment and a profound sense of internal decay?

Show me first an America which has successfully coped with the problems of crime, drugs, deteriorating educational standards, urban decay, pornography, and decadence of one sort or another; show me an America that has pulled itself together and is what it ought to be, then I will tell you how we are going to defend ourselves from the Russians. But as things are, I can see very little merit in organizing ourselves to defend from the Russians the porno shops in central Washington. In fact, the Russians are much better in holding pornography at bay than we are.

Please understand that, for purposes of argument, I am given to overstating a case; and that is one of the reasons why you accuse me of contradiction. If one wants to see both sides of a coin, one has, momentarily at least, to bring out each side in exaggerated relief.

THE SOVIET UNION: THE REALITY

(1977)
Let us see whether we can describe the problem which the Soviet Union does present for American policymakers in these years of the late 1970s.

"WORLD DOMINATION"

"Well, their objectives haven't changed, have they? Don't they still want to achieve world domination?"

This question must have been asked me hundreds of times in recent years.

When, in late 1917, Lenin and his associates came to power in Russia, they did indeed have dreams of early world revolution, in the sense of the revolutionary overthrow of the great capitalist powers of Western Europe, as a consequence of which, it was thought, the European colonial empires would be destroyed and the road opened for the advance of the liberated colonial peoples to economic development under Communist encouragement and leadership. (Whether the United States originally figured in their view of the world as a major capitalist-imperialist power is uncertain. In any case, it soon came to do so.)

These hopes were based on the enormous agony, spiritual and economic, in which European society had become embraced by that fourth year of World War I. This had bred much unrest and even desperation. Masses of people were embittered by the horrible and senseless slaughter. Empires were tottering. Class structures were being undermined. It seemed, from the viewpoint of those who had seized power in Petrograd, that the prospects for revolution in the remainder of Europe were bright. And they did indeed propose to do whatever they could to promote it.

This did not mean that these early Russian Communist leaders proposed to bring revolution about elsewhere solely by the action of whatever armed forces they could assemble in Russia—to bring it about, that is, by invading other countries and imposing Communist regimes upon reluctant peoples. There was a difference between revolution and conquest. Revolution, as they saw it, was something bound to flow primarily from the action of the indigenous revolutionary proletariat in each country. Revolutionary Russia might give to these proletarian forces in other countries such fraternal assistance—moral, material, and military—as it lay within their power to give. But it was never conceived that this assistance should replace revolutionary action by the indigenous proletariat of the countries in question. The role of Russian communism was to assist world revolution, not to create it. The thundering predictions of Lenin—and, later, Stalin—about the inevitability of a final apocalyptic conflict between capitalism and revolutionary socialism, much as they may have suggested to Western minds some sort of final armed struggle between a Communist Russia and the entirety of the non-Communist world, had to be understood in this sense.

Actually, it took no more than three or four years for the leaders of the new Communist regime in Russia to recognize that world revolution, as they had conceived it, was not imminent—that the prospect of it had to be relegated to a future too remote to enter into serious political planning. Nor did they ever really intend to sacrifice their hard-won power in Russia to a quixotic effort to hasten the course of history in this respect. Lenin had once said, to be sure, that if there were a real chance of revolution in Germany, Communist Russia ought to sacrifice itself to bring this about. But this predicated, first of all, a *real* chance of revolution in Germany; and secondly, as time went on and the civil war ran its course in Russia, it became less and less realistic to speak about sacrificing, for the benefit of Communists elsewhere, positions of power won with so much effort and heroism. By 1921 the preservation and development of Communist power within Russia had clearly become the supreme task of the regime. It was to remain that way for a half-century into the future.

The rhetoric of "world revolution" remained, of course. It was basic to the ideology. The thought of the universal triumph of the Marxist outlook, with its obvious political connotations, remained the millennial hope, without which no secular religion (which was what Russian communism really represented) could exist. But it ceased to figure as a serious, immediate goal of policy. From this time on, defensive considerations, flowing from Russia's relative weakness and vulnerability, and related not just to the protection of Russia as a country but also to the protection of the regime vis-à-vis the rest of Russia, were to prevail over aggressive-revolutionary impulses in the minds of those who commanded the destinies of that country.

The Second World War brought significant changes. On the one hand, the spectacle of one great Communist power having to fight side by side with various capitalist powers against another capitalist power further undermined the dream of the final conflict between communism and capitalism. On the other hand, the sudden collapse of both German and Japanese power at the close of the war created unprecedented opportunities for the establishment of the power of the Russian state over large contiguous areas where the recent domination by the Germans and the Japanese had destroyed or decisively weakened indigenous powers of resistance. On all this Stalin capitalized to the best of his ability; and the result was of course the creation of the satellite area of Eastern and Central Europe. This, however, while masked as a gain for "communism," was in reality a revival of traditional Russian power in that region—a nationalist gain rather than an ideological one in the original sense. It represented the satisfaction of regional, rather than global, ambitions on the part of the Stalinist leadership. Furthermore, while it did indeed come to constitute a

new military threat to Western Europe, in the sense that the
establishment of a Russian bridgehead in the very center of
Europe represented a fundamental displacement of the military balance of the continent, it also created new aspects of
vulnerability for the Soviet Union itself and served to heighten,
rather than to diminish, the weight of defensive considerations
in the total pattern of Soviet strategic-political thought.

At the same time, a whole series of postwar phenomena—
the consolidation of non-Communist power in the remainder
of Europe; the advance of moderate socialism or welfare-state
practices in the northern part of that continent; and the success of dissident Communist forces in Yugoslavia and China
—further undermined the dream of eventual world revolution
under Russian Communist auspices. From now on, the Soviet
Union would behave *in the main* as a normal great power, the
traditional concerns and ambitions of Russian rulers taking
precedence over ideological ones in the minds of the Soviet
leaders.

This did not mean that the ideological concepts played no
part at all in the conduct of these men, and above all, in their
words and political gestures. On the contrary, the very existence of the Chinese rival, constantly hurling at Moscow the
charge of betraying true Communist principles, forced Moscow in self-defense to emphasize the rhetoric, and sometimes
even to make the gestures, of revolutionary Marxism. But behind this verbal smoke screen, the men in the Kremlin were
really acting overwhelmingly, so far as international affairs were
concerned, in the tradition of nationalist Russian rulers of
earlier periods. Their predominant and decisive concerns ran
to the protection of their own rule within Russia, and also to
the security of the Russian heartland which served as the indispensable base for their power and with which, for all their
ideological preconceptions, they were indissolubly linked by
the powerful bonds of national feeling.

It will be said, of course: yes, but dreams of world domination and a persistent tendency to expansion, as characteristics of Russian outlooks and actions, were not new to Russia

in the Communist period; they could be observed for centuries in the conduct of tsarist statesmen. And, it will further be asked, as the Communist leaders come to conform more closely to the traditional patterns of Russian statesmanship, will not the original ideological motives for aggressive policies simply be replaced, then, by the more traditional ones?

The point is a good one, and not to be answered in a word. In the period of the Grand Duchy of Muscovy the intolerant religious orthodoxy on which, in part, the grand dukes based their claim to the legitimacy of their power had global implications. It is also true that in both periods of tsarist history— Muscovite and Petersburg—the Russian state showed a persistent tendency to what might be called border expansion, extending its power, time after time, to new areas contiguous to the existing frontiers.

The first of these phenomena had serious significance only in the Muscovite period. It was comparable to the ideological orthodoxy of the Soviet period, but was equally remote from any possibility of realization. For this reason it was, like its latter-day Marxist counterpart, not very important as a guide to action.

The second of the two phenomena—the tendency to border expansion—affected both Muscovite and Petersburg statesmanship, and has indeed manifested itself in the Soviet period as well. (Stalin was highly affected by it.) It thus poses a more serious question. If it does not play a prominent part in the motivation of Soviet leaders today, this is a product, one must assume, of the force of circumstances rather than of natural inclination.

In the West, Stalin left Russia saddled with so vast a glacis —so vast a protective belt—in the form of the satellite area, and this represented in itself so serious a responsibility and in some ways a burden, that there was not only no strong incentive for his successors to expand it (West Berlin being the major exception), but any such effort would have posed considerable danger. On the Asiatic border, the stalemate in Korea (after 1952) and the anxious vigilance of the Chinese made further expansion impossible except at the risk of a major war.

This left only three border regions of any significance: Afghanistan, where, for the moment, the situation was not such as to invite or justify expansionist moves on the Russian side; Iran, where again the risks were higher and the possible profit very small; and finally, the Scandinavian North, where the NATO activity and the naval rivalry indeed provided new defensive incentives for an extension of Russian power but where, again, the NATO involvement meant that any attempt to realize such an extension would involve very high risks of major war.

In these circumstances, the traditional Russian tendency to border expansion has found few promising outlets, and—except in Asia—little incentive in recent years. It may make itself felt again in the more distant future. For the moment it is not a major component in Soviet motivation. It is, in any case, an impulse which is regional, not universal, in character.

There is one last facet of Soviet policy that will perhaps be cited as evidence of the alleged desire to achieve "world domination." That is the extent to which Moscow has recently involved itself with the resistance movements of Southern Africa and with leftist political factions in other Third World countries.

I am afraid that I am unable to see in this phenomenon anything that is particularly new, anything that falls outside the normal patterns of great-power behavior, anything that proceeds from purely aggressive, as distinct from defensive, motives, or anything reflecting a belief that there is a serious prospect for a major extension of Soviet power through such involvements.

The effort to assist to the seats of power in distant countries factions whose aims seem reasonably compatible with one's own is, as I have already noted, not foreign to the normal practice of great powers, including the United States. Why it should cause such great surprise or alarm when it proceeds from the Soviet Union, I fail to understand. The high degree of responsiveness of African resistance leaders to pseudo-Marxist ideas and methods, justifying as these do both heavy bloodshed as a means to the attainment of power and the establishment of a ruthless dictatorship to assure the maintenance of it, presents a powerful invitation to Soviet involvement and one which, incidentally, they can scarcely reject without playing into the hands of the Chinese critics and rivals. Too often, a failure on the Soviet side to respond to such appeals for support is to throw the respective factions into the arms of the Chinese.

In any case, recent Soviet efforts along this line would appear to have been on a scale hardly comparable to our own, and no greater than those of the Chinese. The Russians have known no Vietnams in recent years. They have not even sent their own forces abroad into other countries (the exception being the Eastern European region which we, by tacit consent, assigned to their good graces in 1945)—a measure of restraint which we Americans can scarcely claim for ourselves. And such efforts as they have made to support factions agreeable to their concepts and purposes in Third World countries do not strike me as exceeding, either in nature or in scale, the efforts their Communist predecessors mounted, without inspiring great alarm in American opinion, in earlier decades.

All in all, then, these apprehensions of a Russian quest for "world domination," which have been used to justify appeals for a totally negative, hostile, and militaristic attitude towards the Soviet Union, have little substance behind them and are not responsive to the real profile of the problem which the existence of Communist power in Russia presents for American statesmanship.

THE INTERNAL SITUATION

No Western policy towards the Soviet Union that fails to take into account the nature and situation of the present Soviet leadership can be a sound one. Much of the discussion of Soviet-American relations on the alarmist side is cast in terms indistinguishable from those that were being used at the height of the Cold War, around the time of the death of Stalin. One would suppose, to read this material, that no significant change of any sort had taken place since Stalin's death—that the men now in power presented precisely the same problem from our standpoint as their predecessors of a quarter of a century ago. Actually, this is far from being the case.

The present Soviet leadership is, as governing groups in great countries go, an exceptionally old one. The average age of the top five or six figures is well over seventy. About half the members of the all-powerful Politburo (full and alternate) are upwards of sixty-six years of age. Half the members of the Presidium of the Council of Ministers (the governmental counterpart of the Politburo, which is the supreme *Party* body) are over sixty. The advanced age of the senior leadership in the Soviet Union is a fact well known to all students of Soviet affairs.

This does not mean that the men in question are ineffectual or lacking in the capacity for hard work. It does mean that they are men who have had long and sobering governmental experience. Men of this age and this experience are not normally given to adventuristic policies or to moves likely to impose enormous additional strains and uncertainties upon themselves and upon the system of power they head.

The composition of the Politburo and the other senior bodies of the regime has remained remarkably stable for well over a decade. And this stability has communicated itself to the entire senior bureaucracy—political, military, and economic—a body numbering several hundred people. At the last Congress of the Communist Party, held in March 1976, 90 percent of those elected to the Central Committee, a body in which all the powerful figures of the regime are represented, were being re-elected, which means that they had already belonged to that body for at least five years. Most of them, in fact, had been there longer.

Entry into this senior bureaucracy from lower echelons is, in these circumstances, a rare privilege, and difficult to achieve. Candidates for such promotion are obviously examined with extreme care by the top leadership; and everything known about their personalities suggests that among the qualities that commend them for it are steadiness, balance of view, ability to fit into the bureaucratic machinery, and a quiet loyalty and dependability that does not preclude independent initiative and judgment.

The methods by which these senior echelons of the bureaucracy are kept in line by the top leadership differ radically from those of Stalin. He controlled them by sheer terror and by pitting them one against the other in a struggle for favor where the slightest misstep spelled personal disaster. This assured their slavish obedience but lamed their powers of initiative and their effectiveness as administrators. The present leadership relies on more traditional and conventional means of control: outstandingly the meticulous and judicious distribution of authority, prestige, and privilege.

Now a senior bureaucracy chosen and handled in this way is not something that the top leadership can disregard or push around at will. The mutual dependence is too great. It has to be carefully "managed" (*menagé*, in the French sense). There are limits to the extent to which it can safely be taken unawares by abrupt decisions of the ruling group, or changes of policy for which it would not be prepared and would have no understanding.

I emphasize this, because many of the more alarmist visions of Soviet behavior, as now voiced in the United States, seem to reflect a view of the top Soviet leadership as a group of men who, having all internal problems effectively solved and nothing to do but to plot our destruction, sit at the pinnacle of a structure of power whose blind and unquestioning obedience resembles that of a tremendously disciplined military force, poised for the attack and only awaiting superior orders. This is unrealistic even from the standpoint of the actual relations between that leadership and its own bureaucracy. It is even more unrealistic when applied to the relationship of that leadership with the leaders of the Eastern European satellite regimes. And it disregards another factor commonly regarded in the West as insignificant in the case of Russia: namely, public opinion within the country. Public opinion in Russia naturally does not play the same role in Russia that it plays under a democratic system; but it is not wholly without importance in the eyes of the regime, if only because it affects political and labor morale. The reactions of common people, too, are something the regime has to think about before it launches on abrupt and drastic changes of policy. All this has relevance, of course, to the fears expressed in the West about a sudden Soviet attack on Western Europe, for it affects the ability of the regime to take full advantage of the element of surprise.

The Soviet leadership must be seen, then, as an old and aging group of men, commanding—but also very deeply involved with—a vast and highly stable bureaucracy. This bureaucracy is very much a creature of habit. It is effective in governing the country, but it would not be a very flexible instrument for sudden or abrupt changes. This does not preclude a certain amount of conspiratorial activity on the part of the secret intelligence services and of those sections of the Party which deal with clandestine operations in foreign countries. It does mean that the Soviet apparatus of power is not one that can suddenly be turned around and switched, in the course of a few days, from the normal governing of the country to the huge and wholly abnormal exertions of a major war.

All of the above would be true even if the main concerns of this top leadership were ones addressed primarily to foreign affairs, and specifically to thoughts of aggressive expansion at the expense of other powers. Actually, there is no reason to suppose that this last is the case. The overwhelming weight of evidence indicates that there has never been a time since the aftermath of the recent war when the main concerns of the Soviet leadership have not been ones related to the internal problems that face them: first, the preservation of the security of their own rule within the country, and secondly, the development of the economic strength of a country which, although considerably greater than the United States in area and population, has only roughly one-half of the latter's gross national product.

With respect to the first of these concerns the leadership faces a number of problems—not immediately crucial ones, but ones that give it no small measure of puzzlement and anxiety. One of these is the general indifference, among the population, towards the ideological pretensions of the regime, and the curious sort of boredom and spiritlessness that overcome so much of Soviet society in the face of the insistence of the regime that nothing but that same stale and outdated ideology must find expression in either public utterance or organized activity. This has a number of negative consequences which the regime cannot ignore. Not the least of these is the appalling growth of alcoholism in all echelons of the population but particularly among the working youth. Another one is the continuing vitality of religious faith under a regime which has always held religion in contempt and created its own ideology as a replacement for it.

This situation, in which the populace simply does not have at heart, and indeed is indifferent to, what the regime puts forward as the source of its own legitimacy and the sole acceptable motive power for political and social activity, is an unsettling one from the standpoint of the leadership. It finds an even more unsettling counterpart in the state of affairs which prevails throughout the satellite area of Eastern Europe, where lack of interest for the official dogma is even more widespread, more pronounced, and less concealed. In normal times, all this can be controlled, and partly concealed, by the usual devices of authoritarian power. But it means that the spiritual and political foundation on which Soviet power rests is not entirely a sound one; there are limits to the weight it could be asked to bear.

Then there is, of course, the problem of dissent among the intellectuals. This is probably not as much of a problem as the American press would have us believe. For the reporters in Moscow, the dissidents are close at hand, and their strivings and sufferings make good copy. Actually, the dissidents have few means of appealing for mass support within the country. And their aims are unfortunately somewhat confused by association in the public mind with the cause of Jewish emigration —a confusion for which the Western press, again, has largely itself to blame. Nevertheless, they present a disturbing problem, particularly for a regime which, unjust as are many of the methods it employs to repress dissidence, is unwilling to return to the wholly ruthless and cruel devices of the Stalin era. The dissidents present a problem whether they are kept at home or permitted to emigrate; and the regime appears to vacillate, with much uncertainty, between the two methods of treatment. While their activities are not a serious immediate threat, no fully satisfactory means has been found of dealing with them. And if, with time, their message begins to get through to student youth and to touch those mysterious springs of student revolt which bubble up so suddenly and seemingly unaccountably in all countries, the danger could become more serious. It was, after all, something very similar to this that occurred in the final decades of the last century and laid much of the groundwork for the eventual demise of the tsarist regime.

The concerns just mentioned relate to the state of mind of the Soviet population as a whole. But there is a special dimension to this problem in the form of the strong nationalistic feelings that prevail in certain of the non-Russian constituent republics of the Soviet Union. It was the original pretension of the regime that the Marxist-Leninist ideology would provide the fraternal bond which would unite these peoples with the Russian people and justify their inclusion in the Soviet Union. One of the great tragic problems that has confronted the Soviet leadership ever since the inception of the Russian Communist state has been the fact that in this century national feelings have shown themselves to be more powerful as a political-emotional force than ones related, as is the Marxist ideology, to class rather than to nation. Thus many people in the non-Russian republics who have no great objection to the concepts and practices of Marxist socialism per se experience a strong restlessness by virtue of the subjugation to Russian rule which—to them—their inclusion in the Soviet Union implies. This is aggravated by the fact that in some instances these people have a stronger tradition of individualism generally and of private economic initiative in particular than have the Russians. And its seriousness as a problem for the Soviet leadership is further heightened by the fact that in certain of these republics the population is increasing faster than in Russia proper, so that the balance between Russians and non-Russians in the Soviet Union, already one of approximately half and half, is steadily changing to the disadvantage of the Russian inhabitants of the central heartland.

Like the problem of the dissidents, this national restlessness in the constituent republics is not a serious short-term problem for the regime, but it is a hard one to cope with; for both tolerance and repression tend to enhance rather than to dispel it. If, therefore, the regime does not have to fear it excessively in the short term, it has to recognize that it has still not found the answer to it. And this, too, is disturbing for anyone within the regime who has any historical sense; because the very similar nationalistic restlessness that prevailed among certain of these minority peoples in the tsarist time proved, when that regime came under severe pressure, to be one of the major factors that conduced to its downfall.

Added to these concerns, and probably more important than any of them in the claims they place on the attention of the leaders, are the various continuing problems of the economic development of the country. An enormous amount has been achieved in this respect in recent decades; but there are still problem areas which give rise to serious concern. Chief among these, of course, is the persistent inadequacy of Soviet agriculture to meet the needs of a growing population. This is not all the fault of the mistakes of collectivization; some of it can be traced to the unfortunate oddities of climate and geography with which Soviet agriculture is plagued. But whatever the causes, it is a situation which has not ceased to be a source of grave anxiety to those charged with the task of making the Soviet system work. And beyond this, there are the other problems: technological backwardness (in comparison with the advanced West) in a number of key areas; the inability of the system to create a distribution system for consumer goods that compares with that of Western countries; shortage of proper housing; and the continuing relative inefficiency of labor.

All these factors deserve attention, because they mean that even if the Soviet leaders had wistful ideas of pressing for some sort of a military contest or showdown with the West, they would not wish to proceed in this direction, or even to hasten the arrival of such a situation, until they had progressed much farther than is the case today in the overcoming of these various inadequacies, inefficiencies, and elements of political vulnerability in the situation at home.

THE EXTERNAL SITUATION

Just as the security (not the expansion) of their own power is the prime consideration for the Soviet leaders when they face their own country, so it is when they face the outside world.

This means for them, first of all, no premature or unsettling relaxation of Soviet authority over the Eastern European satellite area. The Soviet leadership could possibly accommodate itself, in time, to a greater degree of independence on the part of one or another of the countries concerned (to a certain extent it has already done so), but only if this does not change the military-political balance in Europe in a manner too detrimental to Soviet military security or prestige, and only if it does not set up liberationist ripples that would carry into the Soviet Union itself. This last is a greater danger than it would have been before 1939, because the extension of the Soviet borders so far to the west during World War II had the effect of bringing into the Soviet Union peoples who are more sensitive to happenings elsewhere in Eastern and Central Europe than are the Russians themselves.

The first requirement of Soviet foreign policy is thus the preservation of the present delicate balance of forces in Europe and, in the absence of any satisfactory arrangements with the Western powers for mutual disengagement or withdrawal in Central Europe, the assurance of the integrity of Soviet hegemony in that region. This, the reader will note, is a strongly defensive consideration.

The second requirement, not addressed to relations with "capitalist" countries, but one which nevertheless belongs in the category of foreign policy, is the protection of the image of the Soviet Union as the central bastion of revolutionary socialism throughout the world, and of the Soviet Party leadership as a uniquely wise and prestigious body of men, endowed with a profound understanding of Marxist principles and enjoying great experience in their application—hence, an indispensable source of guidance for Communist and national-liberationist forces everywhere.

This, obviously, is the ideal, not the complete present-day reality. It is an ideal which has been steadily eroded in recent years, and is still under severe attack by the Chinese and others. But it is not wholly devoid of political substance. It is the pretense, if not the reality, and it must, in the eyes of the men in the Kremlin, be defended at all costs.

Why defended? Because the forfeiture or serious undermining of this image would spell for the leadership the most dangerous sort of isolation and insecurity: isolation between a capitalist world which has not fully accepted it, and could not fully accept it, and a Communist world that had lost confidence in it and rejected it; insecurity, because the loss of this image would throw into question the legitimacy of the regime at home. The posture of moral and political ascendancy among the Marxist and national-liberationist political forces of the world is essential to the justification of the dictatorship exercised over, and the sacrifices demanded of, the peoples of the Soviet Union for more than half a century. Having once forfeited the plausibility of this external posture, it would be hard to maintain the internal one.

This is a situation which will be fully comprehensible, perhaps, only to those who have some idea of the importance that attaches to theory and pretense in the Russian scheme of things—an importance which normally looms greater in Russian eyes than that of the underlying reality. This, in any case, is the reason why the leaders of the Soviet Union could not possibly consider the abandonment of the role of a principled, dedicated force—the leading force, in fact—for the implementation of the ideals of Marxist socialism, and why they cannot do other than to try to protect themselves, by a vigorous show of orthodox Communist verbiage and activity directed to the Third World, against the attacks of the Chinese and other

dissident Communist forces, aimed precisely at the image they
feel obliged to preserve.

This motivation underlies a multitude of facets of Soviet
behavior with relation to the countries of the Third World. It
is not the only motivation that affects that behavior. Military
and economic considerations also enter in. But it is the primary
source of most of those Soviet policies and actions with relation
to the southern continents that arouse so much indignation
and alarm in Washington.

The danger that would be presented for the Soviet leadership by the loss of importance as the center of the Communist
world is not just a political and psychological one. It also has
military-strategic implications of the gravest nature. The loss
of this position, as we have just seen, would mean that Soviet
Russia would fall between two chairs: between a Communist
world that had rejected it and a capitalist world that would not
accept it. And it just happens that the outstanding powers of
each of these two forces, the dissident Communist world and
the distasteful capitalist one, are also, as things stand today, the
powers that pose the greatest military threats to the Soviet
Union: China and the United States. The loss of the image of
leadership among the Communist forces of the world would
thus subject the Soviet Union to a military isolation as well as
a political one.

We have noted the way in which Soviet military power
appears to people in the United States. How does American
military power, in conjunction with other NATO power, appear to the people in the Kremlin?

Let us remember, first of all, that since the Korean War the
Soviet Union has been faced with an American-NATO defense establishment which was in most respects superior to its
own. It has been superior, above all, in nuclear strategic power,
and still is. It has had a superiority in warheads and in missile
accuracy. It has had a superior strategic bombing arm. It has
ringed the Soviet Union with missile bases: in Western
Europe, in Greece and Turkey, in Okinawa and Korea, and I
don't know where else. It has had, particularly when the navies

of the European NATO powers were included, a clear naval superiority. Only in ground-force strength in Central Europe could it be considered inferior to that which the Soviet Union has been able to mobilize against it—and even there, not as much as is commonly alleged.

This is the way things really have been. But let it also be remembered that the way things are is not always the way they appear. There is no reason to doubt that not only do the Soviet strategists not exaggerate the strength of their own power as we do, but they probably do exaggerate, conversely, the strength of ours. The picture I have just painted has to be magnified to some undetermined but surely not insignificant extent to take account of this distortion. I am not sure that even in Central Europe the balance of forces looks to the Russians so overwhelmingly favorable to them as we suppose. The weaknesses of the satellite forces are better known to them than to us, and no doubt loom larger in their scheme of things. And I see no reason to suppose that twenty-nine NATO divisions, eleven of them armored and several of them German, supported with nearly seven thousand so-called tactical nuclear weapons, look to them like the pitiable and hopelessly inferior force they are constantly depicted as being to the Western European and American public. Particularly would this be the case if the strength of the Warsaw Pact forces should be actually, as I suspect, substantially that which the Communist negotiators recently revealed, for the first time, to their opposite numbers in the talks on the Mutual and Balanced Force Reductions. The Western negotiators, who had long demanded these figures, received them with scornful skepticism when they were finally made available. But are we so sure that the error was not in our own exaggerations?

To this it will be said, I know, that all this cannot be a source of serious concern to them, for they know that our intentions are good. Really?

Let us remember that here, too, as in the military field, there is a distortion of the lenses that makes a capitalist government appear—insists, in fact, that it must be—hostile and menacing in its intentions towards the bastion of world communism.

This thesis has been carried forward in a myriad of forms by
the Soviet propaganda apparatus for a quarter of a century. It
is not to be expected that it has had no place at all in the
thinking of the Soviet leaders. The extent to which they believe
their own propaganda is always a question; the one thing that
is fairly certain is that they always believe it *to some extent.*

But beyond this, the Soviet leaders are all aware that there
are forces operating in American political society, as in that of
some of the Western European countries, which are bitterly
and actively hostile to them and would not be in the least averse
to the use of military measures against them, if there were the
slightest prospect of success. They have not forgotten the Captive Nations Resolution, still on the books, which commits the
legislative branch of the United States government to the
overthrow of Communist power everywhere in Russia and
Eastern Europe. They never forget that the strongest continental component of NATO is a West Germany harboring millions of people whom they, the Russians, threw out of their
homes—a West Germany where these refugees and millions of
nonrefugees greatly resent the division of the country, and
resent particularly the measures that have been taken (outstandingly the Berlin Wall) to try to guard East Germany from
the insidious effects of Western influence. The fact that these
measures were the expression of a consciousness of great political weakness on the Communist side makes things no better
from the Soviet standpoint; on the contrary, it increases the
sense of insecurity they experience when they try to translate
political realities into military terms. Finally, they remember
vividly what most Western Europeans seem to have forgotten:
that it was not so long ago that a united Germany—a Germany
only a third stronger, let us say, than the West Germany that
exists today—was able to wreak vast destruction in their country and to penetrate all the way to the Volga and the North
Caucasus while holding off, at the same time, the combined
forces of France and England in the West. Are they, then, to
minimize the potential power of the western two-thirds of
Germany when it is not opposed to but *in association with* not
only the forces of a number of other Western European coun-

tries, including France and Britain, but also those of the United States? To understand the reactions of the Russians, we must credit them with a much longer memory than that of the Western press, and one that does not make light of potential German power.

It may be argued that the Russians should not let themselves be put off by the existence of forces militantly hostile to them in Western societies—that they should look more calmly and deeply at the balance of political forces in the West, from which scrutiny they could confirm that the extremists have never carried the day, that the weight of Western opinion remains strongly opposed to the idea of another war, and that there has never been a time when the NATO governments, collectively or individually, have been disposed to initate a war against them. All this is true. But the reproach to the Russians for not looking at things this way would come with better grace from a Western community that was prepared to look in the same way at Russia—and to observe the same things in the pattern of Soviet political behavior.

All this is said simply to make the point that the Soviet view of the military balance, and of Western capabilities and intentions, is not the same as ours, and that they do not view with complacency the great accumulation of armed men and weaponry arrayed against them, inadequate as this accumulation may appear to many of us.

I have no means of knowing exactly how the Soviet leaders rate the military strength of Communist China, as it faces them across the long Siberian border. I know only that they rate it highly enough to compel them (if the figures obviously emanating from American intelligence sources are to be believed) to keep on that frontier a huge military force: something in the neighborhood of forty to forty-five divisions and close to a million men.

This is a fact of overwhelming strategic significance. How anyone could overlook its obvious implications I fail to understand. For many decades, a standard feature of Russian strategic thinking, tsarist and Soviet, has been the determination to avoid, if in any way possible, a two-front war that would require the splitting of the Soviet armed forces between the European and Far Eastern theaters. One does not need to be a Russian to feel the force of this consideration. The military planners of any great country would react the same way.

Apprehension about the Chinese threat is heightened by the extreme vulnerability of the long Russian line of communications along the southern border of Siberia to the Pacific. Exposed for thousands of miles to flank attacks from the south, squeezed in perilously at one point between the Mongolian border and Lake Baikal, this line of communication presents a tremendous problem for Soviet military planners.

Apprehension is further sharpened by the very high degree of tension and emotionalism that marks both sides of this most curious relationship and could cause minor incidents to blaze up into major ones with great rapidity.

In the face of this pattern of fact, the fears voiced in this country and in Western Europe about the present danger of a surprise Soviet attack against the NATO countries of Western Europe are almost too bizarre to be credible. Aside from all the other evidence that the Soviet leaders have neither the incentive nor the capacity to launch this sort of attack in that region, the situation on the Chinese border would alone be more than enough to preclude all thought of anything of this sort. How, one wonders, do those who bandy these alarmist fantasies picture the Soviet leaders? Do they see them as utterly devoid of any sense of political and strategic realism, or as men who, for some unexplained reason, have taken leave of their senses entirely? It would have to be one or the other.

The present tension between the Soviet Union and China, it may be argued, cannot be counted on to last forever. The quarrel may be composed. Then the Kremlin would be free to pursue its supposed desire to unleash a new world war.

Nothing (as one high Soviet official once observed to me) is impossible, in politics. But some things are improbable, even highly so; and one of them is an early resolution of the Soviet-Chinese conflict—a resolution, that is, of so far-reaching a character that the Soviet government could afford to withdraw the forces it now maintains on the Chinese border and to throw itself into a military action against the West, secure in the confidence that the Chinese would view this action benevolently and would refrain from taking advantage of it. A superficial rapprochement between Moscow and Peking, involving agreements on border problems and trade and accompanied by a number of amicable gestures and polite words, is not at all beyond the realm of early possibility. But the creation of an atmosphere of complete confidence, based on a general mutual understanding with regard to world problems and a consciousness of far-reaching identity of political interests, is something that could scarcely be achieved in anything less than many years, perhaps decades, if indeed it could ever be achieved at all.

The fact is that the interests of these two great countries *do* differ materially in important respects. And the habits of extreme secrecy of deliberation, plus an exaggerated sensitivity in matters of internal security, to all of which both parties are addicted, militate against the early achievement of any firm and reliable understanding between them. A wise Western diplomacy will neither count on the prospect of a Soviet-Chinese war nor will it take fright if Chinese and Soviet representatives begin at some point to say amiable things and to toast each other at banquets. There are deeper and more durable elements involved in this relationship, ones which militate, for both parties, against the costly adventure of major war but also make it virtually unthinkable, now and for many years to come, that either should relax its guard. So long as things are this way, those Western alarmists who try to persuade us that a surprise Soviet attack against Western Europe is a serious possibility, unless we vastly increase our power to deter it, are living in a dream world of their own and are talking about a Soviet leadership many of the rest of us have never heard of.

When the Soviet leaders look eastward, it is not only China they see. They also see Japan, and are well aware of its immense importance. They would like, of course, to assure against too close an association, particularly in the military field, between

Japan and China. Even the American presence in the area is preferable, in their view, to *that*. They are also eager to obtain, and have in part obtained, Japanese assistance in the development of the resources of the Soviet Far East.

There are, however, two formidable obstacles to any far-reaching further development of Soviet-Japanese relations. One is an intangible: the curious emotional preference on the part of the Japanese, built partly of guilt complex, partly of cultural admiration, for the Chinese over the Russians. The second, more specific, is the question of the four southernmost islands of the chain stretching from the Japanese Hokkaido to Kamchatka—islands that the Russians profess to see as belonging to the Kuriles, which are under their control, whereas the Japanese see them as properly a part of Japan.

Moscow could no doubt appreciably improve its relations with Japan were it able to yield on this point. But there is apparently a fear on the part of the leadership that to do so would be to make itself vulnerable to similar demands for readjustment of borders in Europe, where the Soviet Union also appropriated to itself several areas which other governments do not regard as historically or otherwise natural parts of Russia and would like to recover. Particularly sensitive, in this respect, are territories of Bessarabia, where the likely claimant for restitution would be the Communist government of Rumania, and the erstwhile purely German province of East Prussia, half of which was taken by the Soviet Union in 1945 and the fate of which would be of interest to East as well as to West Germany. In its relations with Japan, Moscow is hung up, actually, on the consequences of Stalin's greedy thirst for more territory at the end of the last war. Thus, even in international politics, are the sins of the father visited upon the sons.

In present circumstances, given the relatively minor strength and defensive posture of the Japanese armed forces as well as the close association of Japan with the United States, the Moscow leadership can view its relations with that country with a sort of wary acceptance, if not satisfaction. But it is also aware of the potentially explosive quality of the situation in Korea, and knows that a renewed military conflict between the two Korean regimes on that peninsula could produce incalculable complications, involving China, the United States, and Japan, as well as itself.

This, too, the men in the Kremlin have to have in mind when they design their policies towards the United States and the West. They have to recognize that a major war between Soviet Russia and the NATO alliance would in all probability blow this delicate situation in and around Korea sky-high and have consequences, at present unforeseeable, which could affect Soviet security in the most intimate way.

Then there is, of course, the Near and Middle East.

This is, let us first remember, a region much closer to the Soviet borders than it is to ours. It would be idle to expect the Soviet leaders not to feel their interests seriously affected by whatever happens in that area.

On the other hand, it should also be recognized that, as noted above, they have no active political interests in that area —none, that is, other than those dictated by the strictest considerations of their own national defense—that could conceivably be worth the predictable disasters of a war with the United States. This being the case, they have a vital interest, as we should have, in seeing to it that the internal conflicts of the area do not take forms that would set the two superpowers at war.

In view of the high sensitivity of this region from the standpoint of their military interests, the Soviet leaders would obviously like to have a maximum of influence there, and have tried their best to acquire it. The methods they adopted were not always wise, and have not always been successful. On the contrary, they must, today, feel a very strong sense of disillusionment and frustration as they turn their eyes in that direction. And these feelings must be supplemented by a new element of alarm as they sit by and watch the pouring of these unconscionable quantities of American weaponry into Saudi Arabia and, more disturbing still, into the neighboring Iran. The United States government can consider itself lucky that the Soviet leadership has shown such patience as it has in the face of this reckless procedure, and that it has preferred to wait, and to keep its options open, rather than to move actively to oppose it, as we did in the case of Cuba. But this patience cannot be counted on to endure indefinitely, unless reassurance can be found in the form of some general understanding with the United States with respect to the area in general.

Soviet policy in regard to the Arab-Israeli conflict has obviously been the product of strong differences of opinion within the Moscow political establishment. There would appear to have been those who would not have hesitated to see Israel sacrificed to the cause of a closer Arab-Soviet relationship, if the latter could be obtained this way; and there have been times when, in specific decisions, it looked as though these people had carried the day. At best, it may be said that their influence was sufficient to occasion considerable vacillation and confusion in Soviet policy. But by and large, one has the impression that the Soviet leaders have realized, increasingly, that the destruction of the state of Israel would not only put an end to what is left of their influence with the Arabs but would probably produce a degree of instability in the affairs of the region, not to mention increased involvement of the United States, which could just as easily imperil Soviet interests as serve them.

Such being the case, one must assume that the Soviet leaders would not be disinclined, today, to reach an understanding with the United States and others over the affairs of the region, if this would help to assure that it would not be exploited against them by any other great power and would reinforce the security of their sensitive southern border.

The Soviet leaders view Western Europe, we may be sure, with a troubled and unhappy eye. Its intimate military association with the United States has always been disturbing. Its high living standards provide an uncomfortable comparison with the gray and depressed quality of personal life in so much of Eastern Europe. The lurid quality of its fleshpots and recreations —its very decadence, in fact—tends to unsettle Communist youth, to the extent they are able to learn about it. And the proximity to power of the French and Italian Communist parties is, as we have seen, a decidedly dubious phenomenon from the Soviet standpoint. The failures of those parties are apt to stand as the failures of communism generally in world opinion; whereas their successes, bound to increase their independence, can serve only to diminish Russian authority in the world Communist movement and to increase the size of the already large sector of it that goes its own way.

Well aware that extensive disarray in Western Europe could and probably would mean similar disarray in Eastern Europe, the men in the Kremlin have no desire to see the stability of the situation there severely disrupted. In these circumstances, NATO and the Common Market probably stand out as lesser evils than the visible alternatives, although they cannot say so. Least of all would these men like to see the whole European continent plunged into the extreme and utterly incalculable chaos of a major war. The one thing that would be certain would be that the status quo that emerged from such a war, even in Eastern Europe, would scarcely resemble that which had existed before, even for that portion of the European population that might have survived the holocaust. What ensued might, from the Soviet standpoint, be worse; it is hard to conceive that it could be much better.

East Germany remains, for various reasons, the kingpin of the entire Soviet position in Eastern and Central Europe. For this reason, Moscow is obliged to cling to positions, with relation to Berlin, to the Wall, and to the division of Germany generally, that are bound to stand as impediments to any fully satisfactory relationship to West Germany and to Western Europe. Many of the individual stances and reactions this necessitates are ones that must inevitably be irritating and unacceptable to Western opinion and a burden on Soviet-German relations in particular. They accept this. It should not be confused with a desire on their part to throw Western Europe and much of the rest of the world into turmoil unimaginable by unleashing a new world war. This would be true even if the nuclear deterrent, strategic or tactical, did not exist at all.

The observations above have dealt with the Soviet view of the situations prevailing in those geographic areas that are of greatest importance to the Soviet Union. There remain, of

course, the many and constantly changing problems of the
Third World. Here, political necessity obliges Moscow to try
to keep its hand in as a supportive force for left-wing and
national-liberationist efforts of every sort. But the opportunities, these days, are few. So far has the cause of anticolonialism
advanced that there are not many more worlds to be conquered
in the way of posing as the noble protector of downtrodden
peoples struggling for emancipation from the yoke of the
colonialists. Aside from one or two places, such as Chile, where
there are indigenous regimes that can be opposed on old-
fashioned ideological grounds, there is not much left but the
resistance movements directed to the overthrow of white rule
in Southern Africa. These, in the circumstances, Moscow must
be expected to make the best of. The effort is unfortunate, and
not to be taken lightly. It contributes, of course, to what may
well be an appalling amount of bloodshed and tragedy throughout that entire region. That it will lead to any sort of effective
Soviet hegemony over the nonwhite peoples of the area when
and if they have achieved the slaughter or expulsion of the
whites is not, however, to be expected; and it is improbable
that Moscow itself expects it. It is doing there what it feels, in
the face of the Chinese challenge, it has no choice but to do.
Whether it enjoys the experience, or hopes for much to come
of it in the way of positive political achievement, is doubtful.

SUMMARY

If these considerations have any validity, the position of the
Soviet leadership might be summed up somewhat as follows:

This is an aging, highly experienced, and very steady leadership, itself not given to rash or adventuristic policies. It commands, and is deeply involved with, a structure of power, and
particularly a higher bureaucracy, that would not easily lend
itself to the implementation of policies of that nature. It faces
serious internal problems, which constitute its main preoccupation.

As this leadership looks abroad, it sees more dangers than
inviting opportunities. Its reactions and purposes are therefore

much more defensive than aggressive. It has no desire for any major war, least of all for a nuclear one. It fears and respects American military power even as it tries to match it, and hopes to avoid a conflict with it. Plotting an attack on Western Europe would be, in the circumstances, the last thing that would come into its head.

The most active external concerns of this leadership relate, today, to the challenge to its position within the world Communist movement now being mounted by the Chinese and others. It will consider itself fortunate if, in the face of this challenge, it succeeds in preserving its pre-eminence within the Communist sector of the world's political spectrum, in avoiding a major war which, as it clearly recognizes, would be the ruin of everyone involved, itself included, and in ending its own days peacefully—its members going down in history as constructive leaders who contributed, much more than Stalin and at least as much as Khrushchev, to the advancement of the glory of the Soviet Union and the cause of world communism.

SOVIET-AMERICAN RELATIONS

(1977)

The implications for American foreign policy of what I have said are probably already apparent in their broader outlines; but I shall summarize them, as briefly as I can.

THE MILITARY DANGER

Let us, first of all, divest ourselves of the widespread fixation that our differences with the Russians must someday end in war—or that military strength, in any case, must be the ultimate arbiter of them. A war between the two countries is not inevitable. The Soviet leaders themselves, and outstandingly Brezhnev personally, do not want it. There is nothing in the divergent political interests of the two countries to necessitate or justify it.

If we insist on placing military considerations at the heart of our consideration and discussion of Soviet-American relations, we run a strong risk of eventually bringing about the very war we do not want and should be concerned to avoid. History shows that belief in the inevitability of war with a given power affects behavior in such a way as to cripple all constructive policy approaches towards that power, leaves the field open for military compulsions, and thus easily takes on the character of a self-fulfilling prophecy. A war regarded as inevitable or even probable, and therefore much prepared for, has a very good chance of eventually being fought.

Let us teach ourselves to look at the Soviet problem as a serious political one which has, indeed, military implications, but to bear in mind that these implications are of a secondary, not primary, nature; and let us not be hypnotized by military values to the point where we become blind to the others and fail to develop the hopeful and constructive possibilities of the relationship.

The greatest danger inherent in the existing competition between the Soviet Union and the United States in the military field is not the danger of a Soviet attack on ourselves or on NATO; it is the danger that the momentum of this tremendous and infinitely dangerous weapons race will get out of hand, will become wholly uncontrollable, and will, either through proliferation or by accident, carry us all to destruction. Even as things stand today, the sheer volume—the megatonnage—of nuclear explosives in our hands and in those of our Soviet adversaries is a menace to all mankind. It far exceeds what could conceivably be used to any good purpose, even in defense. It presents, I repeat, by the very fact of its existence, a danger greater than anything involved in the worst political possibilities of East-West relations. Our first task is to bring this situation under control. And this task begins with a restructuring of our own thinking.

THE SALT TALKS

As these words are being written, the SALT talks are about to reopen. This is good, so far as it goes. There cannot be too much in the way of communication between the two governments about the problems involved.

But even the best results that could be expected from these talks are unlikely to be enough. The main reason for this is that the pace of advancement in military technology is faster than the predictable pace of any negotiations of this nature. The technological background against which the instructions to the two delegations would be drawn up would be one that no

longer entirely prevailed at the time they were concluded, so
that any agreements reached would be bound to be partially
overtaken by events.

But there is another and even more serious danger. Talks of
this nature have in the past developed, and must almost inevitably develop, into contests to see how much one could contrive to keep, in the way of nuclear weaponry, and how much
the other side could be brought to give up, as though the entire
purpose of the exercise was simply to get the other party at a
maximum disadvantage. This is probably inevitable, given the
usual positions and the responsibilities of the negotiators on
both sides. But it constitutes, in essence, only another reflection of the assumption of the ultimate supremacy of military
values in the bilateral relationship—the very assumption, that
is, which lies at the heart of the danger. So long as the view
prevails that that party has won, in the SALT talks, which has
contrived to retain a maximum of its own strategic nuclear
power and has compelled the other party to give up a bit more
of its own, I cannot see much progress being made in the
reduction of nuclear armaments.

This is another way of saying that there is not much likelihood that adequate progress will be made in the SALT talks
(adequate, that is, in relation to the depth and seriousness of
the problem) unless those talks are accompanied by at least
some measures of unilateral restraint in weapons developments
on the part of both parties. This should not really be too
difficult. The amount of nuclear destructive power now in
American arsenals is said by the experts to be just about ten
times what was originally calculated to be enough to make no
war worthwhile from the Soviet standpoint. There is simply no
need for all this overkill. Both sides could afford to give up
four-fifths of it tomorrow, and would still retain enough to
serve all useful purposes. A unilateral reduction of 10 percent,
immediately and as an act of good faith, could hurt neither of
them.

But there are other fields, too, not directly related to the
SALT talks, in which the United States could well afford to

change its own position in the interests of a safer and more hopeful situation with respect to nuclear weaponry; and to these I must now turn.

NUCLEAR TESTING

There is no reason at all why the United States should not offer, on the basis of reciprocity from the Russian side, to give up all testing of nuclear explosives, of any sort. Not only would this not seriously jeopardize our defense, but it would put us in a far better position to take the lead in attempting to induce the members of the rapidly growing company of states having a nuclear capability to do likewise.

I recognize that there are a number of people in our military and scientific establishments who are deeply committed to the underground testing of these explosives, and that scientific curiosity has some part in their commitment. But surely, the main purpose of these tests, as now pursued, is to find some gimmick that will suddenly give us an edge over the Russians in the designing and production of the weapons which employ the explosives in question. And this is exactly the kind of thinking that is going to have to stop, if this mad proliferation of nuclear destructive power is ever to be halted and reversed. If the Russians are willing to stop this testing, we should be prepared to do likewise. What is needed at this point is not to find more ingenious ways of detonating these devices but to learn how we can forestall and prevent their detonation in ways that cause devastation to thousands and millions of people.

THE PRINCIPLE OF
"FIRST USE"

I have recounted, in my own memoirs, how, many years ago, in a memo addressed to the secretary of state, I urged

> that before we decide to proceed with the development of the hydrogen bomb, thus committing ourselves and the world to an indefinite escalation of the destructiveness and expensiveness

of atomic weapons, we re-examine once more, in the most
serious and solemn way, the whole principle of "first use" of
atomic weapons or any other of the weapons of mass destruction; and I made it as clear as any language at my command
could make it that if such a re-examination took place, my voice
would be cast most decisively in favor of the abandonment of
this principle altogether.

Today, twenty-seven years later, although the commitment
to first use is now far more deeply imbedded in the theory and
practice of ourselves and our allies than it was then, I see no
reason to go back on this judgment. On the contrary, I am
more convinced than ever that this pernicious theory has lain
at the heart not only of the nuclear weapons race with the
Soviet Union that has brought us all to such a parlous pass but
also of the proliferation of nuclear weapons across the globe
which we are now beginning to witness.

Our concern should be, of course, to achieve the eventual
elimination of the nuclear weapon and all other weapons of
mass destruction from national arsenals at the earliest possible
moment. But it is clear that this will never be done so long as
we ourselves are committed to the principle of first use—so
long as we entertain, and encourage others in, the belief that
never could we in the Western world assure our own defense
except by initiating the use of these weapons or at least basing
our defense plans on such initiation, which amounts to the
same thing.

Only recently, the Soviet government proposed a general
pact to assure that none of the signatories would be the first
to resort to the use of weapons of this nature. This appeal
was issued on the eve of a meeting of the NATO ministerial
council. It was instantly rejected by that body without even
so much as an internal discussion, let alone discussion with
the Russians. So profound now is the commitment to the
idea that never could NATO assure its own defense without
resort to these weapons, and that their use would be justified
to assure that defense, that the proposal was not considered
worth examining.

I must question this reasoning. I see no reason why NATO

could not, if it wanted, assure its own defense in an environment composed exclusively of conventional weapons. It might cost more; it might require a bit higher sacrifice from the respective peoples. Why not? Is the minor convenience that might be derived from escaping these burdens sufficient to overbalance a danger to all the populations of the Northern Hemisphere, indeed to Western civilization itself, greater than any ever before known? Are the comforts of this particular generation so sacred, do they have such weight in the great span of Western civilization of which we are only a small and fleeting part, that the entire progress and survival of that civilization has to be jeopardized to assure them? What egotism!

I saw it argued somewhere in the public prints, the other day, that we must at once strengthen the NATO forces in Europe because as things now stand we might easily be forced to fall back, in the event of a Russian attack, and then our tactical nuclear weapons, having a limited range, might fall on NATO territory already in the hands of the enemy, thus jeopardizing its NATO inhabitants, instead of the populations farther east. How shameful—this thought! As though the people farther east, who might otherwise have been struck by those weapons, were not people—as though it was somehow better and more tolerable for them, women, children, and all, to be burned up than for people who were citizens of a NATO country—as if those Eastern Europeans, ostensibly the objects of our political sympathy, suffered less, or were of such inferiority that their sufferings mattered less in God's sight—and in ours. Was there ever a better example of the corruption worked on people's minds and assumptions by this habit of thinking about war in terms of nuclear weaponry—this concept of holding populations hostage with a view to extorting advantage from their governments?

This, and much more, is involved in the principle of first use. We cannot get away from it: either we approve of mass destruction as a means of warfare regardless of the disasters it holds for much of humanity, our own civilization included, and in implementation of this approval we cling to the principle of first use of these weapons, whether or not they are used against us; or we disapprove of it, in which case we should have the manliness to take the consequences of our feelings and to resolve that we shall not be the first to inaugurate this means of warfare—that we will find other means to assure our defense.

It is clear that we could not now get away from the principle of first use without consulting our NATO allies and making our best effort to persuade them of the necessity of what we are doing. They, even more hopelessly than ourselves (and, unfortunately, with our encouragement), have locked themselves into the belief that they could not possibly defend themselves without resorting to a form of weaponry that would make any real defense a mockery. Well, if so—so be it. The process of disabusing them of the false lessons we have taught them will of course take time. But has the moment not come to make a beginning?

Bear in mind that what is being suggested at this point is not that we should forgo all manufacture of nuclear weapons or all holding of them in our arsenals (though this, too, I should like to see happen) but only that we should not inaugurate the use of them—be the first to use them—in any military encounter. And there is no reason, in the light of the recent Soviet proposal for a pact to this effect, why this renunciation would have to be a unilateral one. The Soviet government has already offered, after all, to join us in such a step.

CONVENTIONAL WEAPONS

The foregoing observations all run, obviously, to the forfeiture of such advantages as we conceive ourselves to enjoy through the cultivation of nuclear weaponry and the commitment to its first use in any serious military encounter. The first objection to this will be that this would leave us hopelessly outclassed in conventional weaponry, and unable, in particular, to defend Western Europe against a Russian attack.

To this, I can only say the following: If a strengthening of our posture in conventional weaponry is really needed, or to the extent it is needed, to assure our ability to meet our commitments to Western Europe and Japan, then that is that, and the added strength should be made available. But there are several reservations.

First, one would like to make sure that the estimates of Russian strength against which NATO's needs are calculated are plausible and realistic and do not contain the sort of exaggeration we have had occasion to note on many past occasions.

Secondly, one would like to be sure that the maximum effort has been made, in the Mutual and Balanced Force Reduction talks and elsewhere, to achieve a general reduction of the Warsaw Pact deployments in Eastern and Central Europe as well as the NATO ones. If any success is to be had along this line, it will probably be necessary at some point to reinforce the more or less public MBFR talks with more private, wide-ranging, and flexible ones.

Thirdly, one would like to be assured that our own military leaders are prepared to make the most of the equipment now available to them instead of designating it as obsolescent and relegating it to the junk piles or selling it to someone else in order to justify demands for fancier, more recent, and more sophisticated items.

Fourthly, one would like to feel maximum improvement has been made in the fighting capacity of our conventional forces, ground, air, and naval, by readjustments in their composition and their deployment. There have been a number of statements emanating from senior and highly experienced military figures to the effect that existing compositions and deployments are not fully suitable: that neither the positioning nor the equipment of certain NATO divisions, for example, is the best they might be; that the United States Navy should have fewer aircraft carriers on station abroad and a greater capacity for seaborne support of American forces overseas, and so on. The layman cannot judge the seriousness of these needs and possibilities. He can only note that the criticisms come from highly qualified people; and he would like to be sure that all possibilities for improvement along these lines have been explored and exhausted before the final bill for strengthening of conventional forces is presented.

Once these requirements have been satisfied, then I can see no objection to whatever strengthening of the conventional forces may be found necessary, provided the determination of necessity is an honest and realistic one. And if this really means that the defense budget cannot be appreciably reduced, so be it.

But then it is also important that this need for strengthening not be argued before Congress and public opinion on the basis of alarmist distortions of the pattern of Soviet intentions and the likelihood of hostile Soviet action. If a proper American defense posture can be had only by the use of such distortions, then it is better, for the moment, not to have it; for such misrepresentations invariably revenge themselves at a later date in the abuse they work on public opinion. Above all, the needs of national defense must not be presented to the American public in such a way as to suggest that a military outcome of our differences with the Russians is the most likely one, and military considerations are overriding in Soviet-American relations. If an adequate NATO defense establishment can be created in Europe only at the cost of persuading people that an armed conflict is ultimately inevitable or that the best we can hope for in East-West relations is a military standoff of indefinite duration based on an atmosphere of total suspicion and hostility, then I am not sure that the effort to achieve such an establishment would not be self-defeating; for no real security is to be attained along that line.

INTELLIGENCE

In the pattern of Soviet-American military rivalry and mutual suspicion, no one will ever know exactly what part has been played by the activities of the secret intelligence services on both sides; but that this part is a very large one is beyond question. I myself have had occasion to see instance after instance in which American intelligence authorities have mounted, or have attempted to mount, operations which have constituted, or would have constituted, a direct abuse not just of Soviet-American diplomatic relations in the formal sense but of the very possibilities for reaching a better understanding between the two governments. And I see no reason to suppose that the Soviet intelligence authorities have lagged in any way behind our own in this respect. A good example of the damage these activities can do will be found in the effect of the U-2 episode, in 1960, on the summit meeting then under contemplation.

One of the most dangerous aspects of these far-flung and extravagant efforts at snooping is that they, like many of the regular military preparations, reflect a pattern of assumptions in which the relationship between the two countries in question is virtually indistinguishable from what would prevail if a state of war already existed or if the early coming-into-existence of such a state of war was regarded as inevitable. But such assumptions, once made the basis for governmental activity on an extensive scale, soon come to take on reality in the minds of those who are called upon to act on the basis of them; and they then have a contagious effect—both on the remainder of the governmental establishment within which they operate and on the one against which they are directed.

A second and no smaller element of danger, inherent in these activities, is the great difficulty of controlling and adjusting them to the needs of a constructive relationship. Their very nature requires that they be known to very few people. Thus many of those in high position who might have the authority and the wisdom to control them cannot do so because they know nothing about them. But beyond this, even where they are known, it is a bold and risky thing for a civilian official, such as a career ambassador, to try to place, or even to recommend, restrictions on them, for he can easily thereby put himself in the position of one who obstructs efforts and operations regarded as necessary to the national defense.

Activities of this nature do not normally enter into the exchanges and discussions between governments, although the discussants often have those of the other party prominently in mind, as causes for suspicion, even as they talk of other things. This, in fact, is a further aspect of the danger that surrounds them. In 1972, to be sure, the great risks of accident then being presented by the mutual shadowing of Soviet and American naval vessels at sea were made the subject of discussion between the two governments, and an agreement was arrived at, useful but very limited in scope, to reduce the danger of collisions. This was, however, a beginning that scarcely scratched the surface of the larger problem to which it related.

It might be thought that a general betterment of the atmosphere of Soviet-American relations would find reflection in a diminution in the intensity and dangerousness of efforts of this nature. Unfortunately, one must expect that if such an improvement were to occur, the operatives of secret military intelligence would be the last to take note of it and to be influenced by it, unless they were to receive specific instructions from their superiors to place limits on their activities.

If the trend towards militarization of the Soviet-American relationship is to be abated and reversed, I see nothing for it but that the governments must take account of this problem, must do what they can unilaterally to temper the recklessness and dangerousness of much of what is now occurring in this field, and must then, at the suitable time and in the suitable forum, find means to consult together with a view to finding further means to curb and control activities of this nature. If war is not really inevitable or even probable, then our lives do not depend primarily on how much we can learn that someone else does not want us to know about his doings, and how much we can conceal about our own.

A total abandonment of secret intelligence gathering (as distinct from secret political operations, which constitute another subject) is not to be expected. It was a normal feature of the policies of national states long before either the Soviet Union or even the United States came into existence; and it would be utopian to hope for its total disappearance. But there are limits. It is one of those instances where, as Shakespeare observed, "Take but degree away . . . and, hark! what discord follows." The problem is not to abolish secret intelligence. The problem is to see that it does not get out of hand, which it has been—both on their part and on ours—in a fair way of doing.

THE DISSIDENTS AND
HUMAN RIGHTS

In the late 1880s a cousin of my grandfather, bearing the same name as myself, wrote, after a long and arduous journey of investigation in Siberia, a book entitled *Siberia and the Exile System* in which he described the sufferings of the political prisoners and exiles who had been sent to that region by the tsarist authorities by way of punishment for their various efforts of opposition—some not very violent, some extremely so— against the tsarist regime. The book was something of a sensation, was translated into many languages (there was even an illegal Russian edition), made a deep impression everywhere, and had a lasting effect, in particular, on the attitudes of the educated Western public of that day towards tsarist Russia. This effect could still be felt, in fact, at the time of the Russian Revolution, in the enthusiasm with which large parts of the Western public welcomed that event.

Twenty years after the Revolution, Russian society, and particularly intellectual society, fell victim at the hands of Stalin and his henchmen to a regime of terror second to nothing ever experienced by any great country in the modern age —a regime many times worse in scale and brutality than anything which the elder George Kennan had ever been obliged to observe. A whole generation of writers, artists, actors, directors, intelligentsia of all sorts, many of them talented people, were swept away, together with millions of other people, in this vast holocaust. Strangely enough, however, while the relatively mild tsarist acts of oppression had produced torrents of protest in Western countries, these terrible purges of the period 1935 to 1939 did not, nor did the equally horrible measures taken during World War II against certain minority peoples of the USSR, and against the populations of certain of the areas overrun by Soviet forces. The victims of *these* persecutions, including such great figures as the poet Mandelstam, went, so far as the Western world was concerned, silently, obscurely, and helplessly to their martyrdom and death.

Forty years have elapsed since that terrible time. The regime now in power in Russia takes measures, too, against those of its citizens who oppose it, who publicly disagree with it, or who make trouble for it in other ways. These measures, like those of the tsar's government nearly a century ago, are often stupid, unfeeling, needlessly brutal, bound to aggravate the very contumacy against which they are directed. In scale and severity,

however, they are incomparably smaller and less horrible than
those undertaken by the Stalinist police system in the 1930s.
The present dissidents, unhappy as is their situation, are
treated—relatively speaking—with a liberality which in Stalin's day would have been unthinkable: permitted to reside, in
many instances, in their homes in Moscow, to write their
dissenting literature and to distribute it privately, to consort
with foreigners, to take their complaints to foreign correspondents and to appeal through them to the sympathies of the
outside world.

I would not like to be misunderstood. I am far from approv-
ing of the treatment these people are receiving at the hands of
the Soviet police. I feel almost sorry for a regime whose sense
of weakness is so great that it cannot find better ways than this
to cope with differences of opinion between itself and a relatively small and helpless band of intellectuals. But honesty
compels me to note—and I think my readers should note—
that compared with what existed forty years ago, what we have
before us today, unjust and uncalled-for as it may appear in our
eyes, is progress. And yet it is the object of Western press
attention and Western protests on a scale far more extensive
than were the much greater excesses of the Stalin period. The
new American administration even finds itself faced with demands, from both outside and inside its own ranks, that it
should go much further and should make the treatment of the
dissidents the decisive touchstone of Soviet-American relations
—if necessary, to the detriment of progress in other areas of
the relationship.

What conclusions, one wonders, are the Soviet leaders to
draw from this state of affairs? Are they expected to conclude
that although greater mildness in the treatment of dissidence,
in comparison with the Stalin period, has now led to a marked
increase in foreign indignation and protest, further mildness
will have the opposite effect, causing oppositionist activities in
Russia to subside and taking the heat off the Western reaction?
Or are they going to conclude that Stalin was essentially right
after all—that the only way to maintain a firm Communist
dictatorship and to make the Western world accept it is to

punish dissidence as Stalin did: with such prompt and fearful terror that the Western press never even hears about the sufferings and fate of the victims? Are they going to conclude, finally, that they were wrong to relax as much as they *have* relaxed, that a mile will be taken wherever an inch is given, and that to yield further would be to embark on a path that would lead eventually to the destruction of the regime itself?

In this, Western policymakers have the heart of the dilemma; for while a little pressure from Western opinion may be useful, too much of it can cause the Kremlin to feel that what is at stake for it is self-preservation; and then there will be no question of yielding, for self-preservation is a consideration that would take precedence over any other considerations, all the rest of Soviet-American relations included; and where there is no question of yielding, there will be no benefit brought to those on whose behalf these protests are being made—only harm to United States-Soviet relations.

The Soviet government asked for trouble, of course, when it signed the Helsinki declarations on human rights. The Western governments are formally on good ground in making this an issue of their relations with Moscow, if they care to do so. But the question remains whether it is wise for them to proceed much farther along this path: whether this will significantly benefit the people on whose behalf they are being asked to intervene; and, if so, whether this benefit will be of such importance as to outweigh the progress that might, in other circumstances, be made in other fields.

I should perhaps explain that I yield to no one in my admiration for such men as Solzhenitsyn and Sakharov; I would place them among the greatest Russians of the modern age. Were I a Russian, they would have my deepest gratitude and, I suppose (it is always dangerous to think you know how noble you would be in hypothetical circumstances), my support.

But I am not a Russian. Neither are all those for whom the United States government professes to be the spokesman. I have tried, in this book, to place myself in the position of the United States government, to look at things from the standpoint of its responsibilities, and to establish something resembling priorities between these various responsibilities where they conflict.

Among those responsibilities, the task of overthrowing the Soviet government, or bringing about a fundamental change in its nature, does not, as I see it, figure. There are limits to what we can put upon ourselves. It is enough for us to find our own way out of the labyrinth of problems in which the modern age is enveloping us and to create conditions within our own country with which we can profess ourselves satisfied. With relation to the Soviet government, our task is not to destroy it or make it into something else but to find means of living side by side with it and dealing with it which serve to diminish rather than to increase the dangers that now confront us all.

General George Marshall used to say to those who worked for him: Don't fight the problem. I have been going here, and I think the United States government must go, on the theory that the problem, in this case, is the Soviet government as it is, as we find it, and as it is probably going to continue to be for some time into the future. I have never advocated an American policy aimed at its overthrow—have in fact actively opposed such a policy—not because the form of government prevailing in Russia commends itself to my tastes and sympathies but because I do not think it our business to try to determine political developments in other countries, because we would probably not be able to do this even if we wanted to, and because we would not know what to put in the place of the present Russian regime even if we succeeded in overthrowing it. I know of no potential democratic Russian governments standing in the wings.

Now, we may not see an American governmental policy which includes support for the Soviet dissidents as one aimed at the overthrow of Soviet power. Not all of the dissidents see their own activity that way. It may be argued that what is involved here is not an effort to overthrow that power or to change its fundamental nature but rather to make plain the strength of American sympathy for those who suffer from its excesses, and the warmth of the American desire to see its practices conform more closely to the universal ideals of tolerance and respect for what have now come to be known as human rights.

To this, on principle, no objection can be raised. The American sympathies in question really exist. There is the Soviet signature beneath the Helsinki declarations. There can be no objection, surely, to the expression by responsible American officials of their hope, and the hope of those they represent, that these undertakings will someday find recognition not just in the words but also in the policies and practices of the Soviet government.

I will go even further. It would not be unreasonable for the United States government to make it clear to its Soviet counterpart that so long as there continue to exist the conditions of which we are being daily reminded by the foreign press corps in Moscow—so long, in other words, as the Soviet police authorities continue to overreact and to proceed stupidly, unfeelingly and with brutality against men and women whose only offense has been to voice, in restrained and unprovocative fashion, views divergent from those to which the regime is, and has been for sixty years, committed—so long as things are this way there will be, and must be, limits beyond which Soviet-American relations cannot develop, limits to the extent to which Americans, either in their personal capacity or through their government, could ever associate themselves with Soviet purposes and ideals, as revealed in present Soviet practice. So long, in other words, as these conditions persist, there must always be maintained a certain distance between the two governments—a distance which no summit meetings, no warm toasts, no friendship societies, no cultural cooperation, and no talk of coexistence can overcome—a distance which, considering the immense responsibilities that rest on both governments from the standpoint of preserving world peace and designing a safer and better world, can only be called tragic. This is the way things will have to be; and for this the Soviet authorities must hold only themselves to blame.

On the other hand, what is most important about many things that are done in international life, as elsewhere, is not *whether* they are done but *how*. There are ways and ways of making plain to the Soviet leaders and to the world how America reacts to the reports of the treatment of the dissidents. Some criticisms are useful; some destructive. Pressures to a given point may yield results; pressures beyond that point may be self-defeating.

The task of the United States government will be to see how these feelings of the American people can be communicated to the Soviet government in a way that will help, rather than damage, the fortunes of those to whose strivings and sufferings they are addressed. But this government will also have to be concerned to see that these expressions of sympathy do not take forms that are misinterpreted in Moscow as direct efforts to shape the course of internal political developments in Russia, and that they do not, in this way, interfere with the completion of the main task of American statesmanship with relation to Russia, which is, as noted above, to reduce the danger posed for both countries and for the world by the present military rivalry.

TRADE

The Soviet government has always attached, and continues to attach, great importance to the possibilities for the development of Soviet-American trade. The reasons for this are no doubt various. They include such practical considerations as a desire to tap America's rich resources of advanced technology, the need for heavy importations of American grain to make up domestic agricultural deficiencies, and so on. But there has also always been a curious feeling on the part of Soviet leaders that a willingness to expand trade, or at least to make public gestures in that direction, is a symbol of a desire to strengthen political relations, particularly in the case of a capitalist country, and therefore has high political significance.

It is difficult for the United States government to respond to such a view. It does not control trade, and cannot, for the most part, increase or decrease it. The trade has to flow, for better or for worse, from whatever commercial incentive can be given to private traders.

Despite the obvious asymmetries between a state trading system, on the one hand, and a system of private trading initiative such as we have, on the other, there is no reason why we should wish to discourage trade with the Soviet Union, provided only that it does not lead to so high a degree of dependence of individual American firms, or groups of firms, on Soviet orders that it would give to the Soviet trade monopoly an undue influence in our affairs, as our oil dependence has given to the Arabs and others, and provided the Soviet Union is not permitted to acquire, through normal trading transactions, access to sophisticated American technology which would have military value and which we would not normally, as a matter of governmental policy, have made available to it. Of this last, our government has to be the judge; and it should see that such transfers of technology do not occur. But here, one should be very sure: first, that the technology in question really is of high and sensitive military value, and could not be produced in the Soviet Union; and secondly, that the Russians could not obtain it from other sources. It will be found, I believe, that the area of technology that could meet both of these criteria is very narrow indeed.

Beyond these rather elementary precautions there is, I repeat, no reason to discourage Soviet-American trade. The idea that trade promotes useful human contacts and conduces to good will and peace can easily be carried too far, particularly when it concerns trade with a foreign governmental trade monopoly. But if it does not do a great deal of good, psychologically and from the standpoint of human contacts, it also does not do any great harm; on the contrary, it is probably mildly useful in convincing people on both sides that their opposite numbers are human beings, not monsters, and that we all live in the same world. In addition to which there is the often forgotten fact that it is economically useful.

In these circumstances, I can see no reason whatsoever why most-favored-nation treatment should be withheld in the case of the Soviet Union. The withholding of it as a device for putting pressure on the Soviet government in the question of Jewish emigration has been obviously unsuccessful—so much so that the case for its abandonment need no longer be seriously argued. And other justifications for this practice are not apparent. The trade has been massively in our favor in recent years; so protectionist considerations are scarcely relevant.

There have been suggestions that we should withhold most-favored-nation treatment, and indeed discourage trade itself, as a means of extorting political concessions generally—that we should not permit grain exports to proceed, for example, unless the Soviet Union consents to give us concessions in other, and unrelated, fields. This idea seems to me to be quite unsound; it is in any case impracticable. When the Soviet trade monopoly enters the American market as a buyer, it pays, or should pay, the going price—the market price, that is—for whatever it buys. If the American seller does not demand more, and consents to sell at that price, and the Soviet trade monopoly then pays it, it has a right to assume that it has done all that could reasonably be asked of it as a trader, and has a right to take possession of the goods for which it paid. We cannot then logically come along afterwards, as a government, and say in effect, "You must pay for this all over again in the form of this or that political price, before you can have the goods." Either we believe in free enterprise and the validity of the market or we do not. If we do, we should concede that to pay the going price is payment enough. If we do not, then we should establish a governmental trade monopoly ourselves and conduct trade for political reasons.

The view that trade with Communist countries (because this affects not Soviet Russia alone) should be used as an instrument for extorting political concessions implies, first, that we do not really need the trade for economic-financial reasons—that we, as a country, derive no significant commercial profit from it and can easily take it or leave it; and, secondly, that for us to consent to trade with another country represents some sort of an act of grace on our part, for which the other party should be willing to pay both the usual commercial price and a political premium as well. Neither of these implications will stand in the case of our trade with the Soviet Union: the first will not because the balance in our favor, averaging several hundred million dollars a year in recent years, is by no means a negligible factor in the calculations of a country which has a balance-of-payments problem; and the second, because it will simply not be accepted there or anywhere.

We may as well accommodate ourselves, therefore, to letting Americans trade with the Soviet Union wherever they find it profitable to do so, conceding most-favored-nation treatment to the Soviet exports to this country, and merely keeping a watchful eye open to assure that sensitive military technology is not unintentionally revealed in this way and that undue relationships of dependence on the Soviet trade monopoly do not develop. The resulting involvements will constitute a certain small anchor to windward in the tenser moments, and we should both profit from the exchanges.

I see, on the other hand, no reason why we should extend extensive government credits beyond those that would fit the pattern of the normal operations of the Export-Import Bank. The Soviet Union has formidable financial resources of its own —sufficient to enable it to conduct in various parts of the world political operations, including massive arms shipments, which we find unhelpful to world political stability. I can see no reason why we should assist it along this line. To which must be added the reflection that the Soviet authorities have never been very forthcoming about their own financial situation. Something in my own Scottish ancestry rebels, I am afraid, against the suggestion that you should lend large amounts of money to someone else whose actual financial situation is assiduously concealed from you.

CULTURAL RELATIONS

At the height of the Nixon-Kissinger détente—in the period 1972–1974—a number of bilateral intergovernmental agreements were concluded between the Soviet and United States governments for cooperation in various fields of science, technology, and public health. In addition to these, there are agreements between private institutions in the United States and various Soviet institutions, involving exchanges of one sort or another.

In the many criticisms that have recently been levied against détente, these agreements and their consequences have been generally forgotten; one gains the impression, in fact, that most of the critics have never heard of them, or consider them insignificant.

Actually, the results of these agreements are not insignificant, nor are they, on balance, negative. Certain of the contemplated exchanges and other forms of cooperation have run into initial difficulties, usually due to unfamiliarity of the Soviet side with cooperative efforts of this nature, sometimes to bureaucratic hesitations and timidities of one sort or another. In addition, certain agreements in the commercial field have remained unimplemented as a consequence of the failure of the commercial agreement of 1972 to gain congressional ratification in Washington. But by and large, the Soviet authorities seem to have tried, in good faith, to carry out their end of these arrangements. Some, especially the agreements in the field of public health and the various arrangements for academic exchange, have proved strongly beneficial. Two hundred scientists (one hundred from each side) are collaborating, for example, on medical research; and Dr. Theodore Cooper, assistant secretary for health, education, and welfare, has expressed publicly the view that American research in this field gained importantly from the experience. All in all, there is no reason to doubt that as initial hesitations are overcome and familiarity grows with the attendant procedures, significant results will be achieved for both sides.

Certain of the agreements are criticized from the American military and hard-line side, on the grounds that the Russians get more information about us out of them than we get about them. This charge obviously reflects a view analogous to that referred to above in connection with negotiations on the control of armaments: namely, that their gain can only be our loss and vice versa—that the purpose of the American side in these agreements is to see how much information it can gain from the Soviet side and how little it can contrive to give up in exchange.

Of this it can only be said that if this—the gathering of military or quasi-military intelligence—was really the purpose our people had in mind in concluding these agreements, it would have been better not to conclude them in the first place. But I see no reason to suppose that it was. The greatest benefit we derive from these arrangements lies in the field of the intangibles: the greater mutual acquaintance between experts on both sides of the line; the breakdown of unreal stereotypes in the minds of both parties; the discovery that not all those on the other side are inhuman and that we actually have a good deal in common. The effect of the agreements in this respect should not be underrated. The number of experts exchanging visits in this way has risen by at least 300 percent since the agreements were pursued, and is now running at two to three thousand per annum in both directions. The positive results of such exposure to the people and surroundings of the other country are of course not immediately visible, and cannot be measured just in terms of the information derived by our side. But the information the Russians obtain from us by this means is, as a rule, information they could obtain from other sources if they wanted to; whereas these intangible benefits which we particularly value are ones it would be difficult to produce in any other way.

Beyond this, it takes a rather smug and provincial view of this relationship to assume that we have nothing to learn from professional contacts of this nature other than such technical information as we can extract from our opposite numbers. We are human beings ourselves, supposedly, as are they; and who is to say that we could not enrich our own way of looking at things by a thoughtful and serious attention to theirs? The fact that their system may not appeal to us is no reason why their experiences and reactions, as human beings, could not be informative, and could not shed some light on our problems.

Naturally, cultural relations, like other ones, must be a two-way street if they are to be fruitful; and if there were reason to believe that the Russians were viewing them from a standpoint of total cynicism and surrounding them with such restrictions and conditions that the direct benefits, from the substantive side, were negligible, and the intangible ones nonexistent, I would be the first to urge their termination. I see no evidence of such an attitude in what I can learn of the operation of the agreements now in force. And until such evidence is forthcoming, it seems to me that this, one of the few potentially constructive aspects of the relationship, should not be forgotten, ignored, or lightly sacrificed to totally unconstructive undertakings.

PROFESSIONALISM AND THE
MOSCOW EMBASSY

Effective diplomacy is not just a matter of grand strategy. It is also a matter of the information and advice one seeks, the people one uses, and the channels for communication one selects for the implementation of policy. In all these respects the practices of the United States government in recent years, in relations with the Soviet Union, have left a good deal to be desired.

There can be no question but that the American political establishment has a long-standing, almost traditional aversion to professionalism in diplomacy. The principle on which it proceeds is that experience in any other conceivable walk of professional life—the law, business, journalism, you name it— would obviously be a better qualification for senior responsibility in the diplomatic field than experience in the Foreign Service itself.

It is not my purpose here to polemize against this concept in its wider application. But it strikes me as being particularly questionable when applied to our relations with Russia; and I believe that our government, by adhering to it, is depriving itself of some of the most valuable resources that lie at its disposal.

If I am not mistaken, there has not been a time since the termination of the ambassadorship of the late Llewellyn Thompson when the American Embassy in Moscow has been used to any significant extent either as a source of information and day-by-day advice for high-level policymaking, or as a channel for the presentation of Washington's point of view and the explanation of its policies to the appropriate levels of officialdom in Moscow. On one occasion our ambassador was excluded not only from personal participation in negotiations highly relevant to his official responsibilities but even from access to adequate information about what was going on.

There seems to have been a belief in Washington that information about Russia could better come through other channels than the regular diplomatic ones; that those charged with the conduct of foreign policy in Washington were in no particular need of professional advice, especially from the field; and that the task of explaining Washington's position to people in Moscow could safely be left to occasional visits by high-ranking American figures to Moscow, to chance encounters by those figures with their Soviet opposite numbers at international gatherings, or to discussions with the Soviet ambassador in Washington. Aside from all questions of personality, this view embraces some serious functional miscalculations.

By failing to use the American Embassy, senior policymakers in Washington are simply wasting the services in Moscow of the men who, of all those who are concerned with the problem of Soviet-American relations, are closest to the problem, live daily in constant exposure to the source of it, follow the situation from day to day, are sensitive to divergencies between the external rhetoric and internal reality in Soviet policy, and have a feel for all that is involved. Most of the officers of that diplomatic mission know some Russian and have had special training of one sort or another for their work —not as much training, to be sure, as they ought to have, because Washington does not give it to them, but more than the great majority of those whose voices are customarily heard in policy formulation. It is painful to see prominent and influential congressional figures sitting humbly at the feet of visiting Russian dissidents in the search for information about Russia, when people far more detached, better schooled in American interests, and better equipped by motivation to tell them what they ought to know never even meet a member of Congress. Some of these dissident figures are of course great men; but it is not the interests of the United States—sometimes not even those of world peace—that they have at heart; and much as they may know about internal conditions in Russia, they are often the merest children when it comes to the understanding of international relations.

By failing to use the Moscow embassy as a channel for informing Soviet officialdom of Washington's views, one deprives that mission of much of its potential value as a source of information on Soviet outlooks and policies; for no more in diplomacy than in any other walk of life is something normally given for nothing; and Soviet officials are not going to be greatly interested in discussing American policy with American representatives in Moscow who are themselves very poorly informed with regard to it.

But beyond this, the task of making Washington's views known in Moscow and gaining understanding for them on the part of Soviet officialdom is not one that can be adequately performed by sporadic encounters between various personalities at the most senior levels. Not only are the senior American figures concerned not always cognizant of the real meaning and background for the words and expressions used by their Soviet opposite numbers, even when faithfully translated, but there is also the fact that Washington's point of view, if it is to be effectively presented, has to be put currently, almost daily, to people in the official Soviet establishment, has to be put by persons who know how to put it, linguistically and otherwise, and has to be put not just at one level but a variety of them —something which the embassy, with its wide set of contacts, is uniquely capable of doing.

A wise American diplomacy with relation to the Soviet Union will be concerned to improve the professional resources it has to help it with this problem, and will then see to it that such resources as it has are used, not neglected.

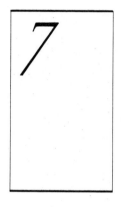

SOVIET
STRATEGIC
OBJECTIVES

(1978)

The following statement was submitted to the Senate Foreign Relations Committee in response to a series of questions put to Ambassador Kennan and others in connection with a study published by the committee in December 1978.*

The questions put to contributors were:

What security objectives underlie Soviet strategic and conventional force policy?

Do Soviet leaders believe their forces are adequate to their objectives?

How do Soviet leaders assess trends in the strategic and theater balances?

In what manner is the Soviet Union likely to use its power?

Are there any circumstances in which the Soviet Union could initiate hostilities against us or our allies?

Would major unilateral steps by the United States to alter the strategic or theater balance significantly change these prospects?

As is well known, anxieties have recently been voiced in a number of Western quarters over the scale and pace of development of the Soviet armed forces, this being perceived as of such dimensions as to be inexplicable by defensive motives

---

*Mr. Kennan's statement appears at page 335 of *Perceptions: Relations Between the United States and the Soviet Union,* published by the Superintendent of Documents, United States Government Printing Office.

alone, and hence indicative of offensive intentions of one sort
or another.

Leaving aside the question of the statistical basis for these
reactions, on which it is not intended to comment in this
paper, the anxieties in question also raise the subject of the
ways in which the Soviet leadership might, or might not, see
it as ideologically justifiable and politically useful for them to
commit Soviet armed forces to action against those of other
powers. On this subject a few observations might be in order.

The ideological postulates which the present Soviet leaders
have inherited from their predecessors (and which have a
greater validity in their eyes than is often supposed) envisage
three ways, and only three ways, in which the Soviet armed
forces might be conceivably and justifiably committed, by deliberate decision of the leaders, to international combat. One
would be, of course, for defense of the Soviet Union, or what
it views as its orbit, in the face of invasion or aggression by a
foreign power. A second would be by way of support for a
"proletarian" faction striving, by means of civil war, to overthrow a "capitalistic" government and social system in one of
the advanced industrial countries and to replace it by a "socialist" one. The third would be by way of similar support for a
"war of liberation"—for what they might see, in other words,
as an effort by a revolutionary faction in a Third World country
to cast off the colonial authority or pseudocolonial influence of
one of the non-Communist advanced countries of Europe or
North America.

This does not imply that the leadership would feel *obliged*
to commit Soviet forces to combat in the last two of these cases
(indeed, in many past instances it has not done so). It merely
means that if it chose to do so, the ideological justification
would be at hand. It also does not mean that it would be viewed
as justifiable, in these cases, that Soviet forces should assume
the main burden of the task at hand. It is clearly implied, in
all authoritative Communist ideological pronouncements, that
such action by Soviet armed forces would have to be of a
secondary and incidental nature, designed to assist, but not to
replace, the basic thrust. This last would have to be delivered
by the respective indigenous faction. The concept of such a

civil war or "war of liberation" being conducted exclusively or even mainly by the Soviet armed forces, on Soviet initiative, in the face of general indifference or passivity on the part of those who are supposed to be the beneficiaries of the action, would be in conflict with the basic tenets of Communist doctrine, which see useful social and political change as flowing primarily and necessarily from the spontaneous action of the "oppressed masses" of the country concerned.*

Beyond this, Communist ideology does not envisage any use, on Soviet initiative, of the Soviet armed forces for actions outside the country. This thus leaves no room, by implication, for the unprovoked initiation of hostilities against another great power.

Now it is indeed true that ideology, while of more than negligible importance for the Soviet leaders, is highly flexible, so that there are few military actions these leaders might wish to initiate for which some sort of ideological rationalization, however flimsy and implausible, could not be found. But the lack of any clear ideological justification for an unprovoked attack on another power just happens to coincide with certain pragmatic considerations which could be expected to commend themselves strongly to the men in the Kremlin. Their outlook would differ from that of many people in the West in that they would not be likely to view military victory, however complete, as an aim in itself, alone justifying a major military effort. Victory, in this sense, would appear to them, not as the end of something, but rather as a beginning—the beginning of something more important, in fact, than military victory alone: namely, the further course and direction of political life in the country in question; and they would normally like to have some reasonable assurance how that was going to develop before taking upon themselves the enormous risks and burdens of another world war. They will not have failed to observe that within fifteen years after World War I Germany, ostensibly the defeated party in that conflict, was again by far the strongest power in Europe; nor will they be unmindful of the fact that

---

*None of this, of course, bars the Soviet leaders, any more than it does the rulers of other countries, from using surrogate forces, or profiting from their spontaneous operations, where opportunity presents itself.

today, thirty years after World War II, the two principal "defeated" participants in that war, Germany and Japan, are enjoying unprecedented industrial and material success under the rule of governmental systems not at all agreeable to Soviet preferences and interests. Before launching another great war they would wish to be assured, therefore, that they would have some means of capitalizing on an eventual Soviet military victory in a way that would represent a permanent advancement of their interests and of those of that part of the international Communist movement that accepts and respects their leadership.

There are, however, only two ways in which this could conceivably be assured: first, by direct Soviet occupation and military government over an indefinite period of time; or, secondly, by the installation in power, in the respective country, of a Communist party strong enough to maintain its rule successfully and firmly over a long period of time, and sufficiently loyal to Moscow to assure that it would continue to respect Soviet leadership even if and when this conflicted with its own political interests and those of the people over which it presided.

In terms of the situation which now confronts the men in the Kremlin, these requirements would be difficult ones to meet. The possibility of direct and permanent Soviet military rule would have to be discarded. Any attempt to rule Western Europe, or the United States, or China, or Japan, by the devices of occupation and military government would clearly exceed the respective capabilities of the Soviet Union, in manpower and otherwise—capabilities already severely strained just by the necessity of garrisoning (not occupying or governing, which would place far higher demands on trained manpower) certain countries of Eastern and Central Europe. Actually countries and areas as vast as those just mentioned, with the possible exception of Japan, are simply not susceptible to total occupation by any foreign power; the task is too vast.

For the Soviet leaders, the decision to launch another major war would have to depend, then, not just on the prospects for military victory but also on the prospective availability of a local Communist faction in the enemy country which would answer to the requirements just outlined and which could be installed in power, like those of Poland and East Germany after the last war, by action of the Russian forces. As of the moment, it is difficult to see where such parties could be found. In the United States a Communist party loyal to Moscow can scarcely be said to exist; and what little there is that could be so described would be hopelessly inadequate, numerically and otherwise, as the basis for a governing apparatus. In China, the existing party would be fanatically committed against Soviet leadership, and would be simply unavailable as a possible instrument for Soviet power. In Western Europe there are indeed two parties, the French and Italian, strong enough in numbers to serve such a purpose; but they are of doubtful reliability today, and would be even more so were they to occupy the seats of government in their respective countries, because their command of the human and physical resources of those countries would then be bound to increase their effective independence vis-à-vis Moscow, and they would be too remote from the centers of Russian power to be kept under control by sheer military intimidation, as are the Warsaw Pact countries today. Even assuming that a Russia which became involved in an aggressive war against any of the great countries or areas just mentioned was successful in the military sense (and it takes a wide imagination to picture anything that could correspond to the concept of "victory" in a conflict between nuclear powers), it would face severe, and essentially insoluble, problems in the effort to capitalize politically on even the most complete military victory. Of none of this will the Soviet leaders be unaware.

To say this is not to say that the Soviet leadership has been, is at present, or will be unaffected by those deeply rooted impulses which have led Russian regimes of all ages to try (and not without impressive success) to expand the area under their control by low-risk encroachments of one sort or another along their lengthy borders, at the expense of immediate neighbors. In the case of the Soviet leadership, it is not inconceivable that this tendency to gradual border expansion might take the form of actual hostilities against a small neighboring country (as in the case of Finland in 1939) if it were thought that the resulting conflict could be isolated internationally and would not cause instability in other areas of Soviet concern. But the Soviet leaders would be disinclined to undertake anything of this nature, whether in the form of minor border encroachments or of hostilities against a small and weak neighbor, if there were a serious danger that this:

(a) might bring into play relationships of military alliance which would lead to war with one of the great powers;

(b) would create serious instability in other areas within the Soviet orbit (as, for example, an attack on Yugoslavia would be likely to do); or

(c) could be easily capitalized on or taken advantage of by a formidable neighbor on another front (as might be expected to be the case with China in the event of any serious Soviet military involvement on the European side).

Thus the traditional Russian predilection for piecemeal border expansion through relatively small and low-risk steps, while not foreign to the inclinations of any Russian regime, finds definite limits, of which the Soviet leaders will not be unaware, in the realities of the present world situation.

The considerations set forth above would be compelling even in the absence of considerations of internal policy acting in the same direction. But actually, such internal considerations are not at all lacking. The most important of them relate to the prospects for Russia's social and industrial development in the remaining years of this century. This is not the place to detail the needs in question. Suffice it to say that the program of social and industrial development on which the Soviet leaders have set their hearts and to which they have committed themselves in the most serious way is still far from complete; and its completion, in view of the long lead time required for major undertakings in this field, could not be reconciled with the preparations for any major military undertaking. Commitment to the decision to launch another world war, even at a point some years in the future, would conflict flatly with the requirements of this program. And there is no indication whatsoever (in fact, there are many indications to the contrary) of any disposition on the part of the leadership to carry out such a reversal of priorities as to signify the abandonment of this program or to remove it from its commanding place among the purposes and preoccupations of the regime in its entirety.

In addition to which it must be noted that the political situation of the Moscow leadership with relation to the satellite countries of Eastern and Central Europe is one of considerable potential fragility; and that any disturbance of the stability of that region could, in view of attitudes and reactions on the part of the non-Russian nationalities of the Soviet Union proper, easily affect the stability of the system at home. The leaders would thus be obliged to bear in mind, in considering any possible inaugurating of hostilities, that any major disturbance of the political status quo in Europe, such as could be expected to flow from a major military conflict, could have serious, and for them dangerous, repercussions on the entire eastern portion of the European continent, not excluding the Soviet Union itself.

All this is also not to say that there is no danger at all of war, involving the Soviet Union, in the years just ahead of us. There remain, of course, the ever-present possibilities of war by inadvertence: by miscalculation, by misread signals, by unacceptable challenges to prestige, by exaggerated anxieties and panic. Viewed from this standpoint, it should be recognized that there are several situations in the world, outstandingly those in Korea and in the Near and Middle East, not to mention Southern Africa, out of which serious military complications, involving any or all of the great powers, are far more likely to arise than from any deliberate decision of the Soviet leadership to inaugurate hostilities against another power.

But it remains to be noted that the danger that complications in the areas just mentioned might lead to general war will be strongly affected by the degree to which the atmosphere of East-West relations, and particularly of Soviet-American relations, is or is not militarized—the degree, that is, to which the tendency to view a great military conflict as inevitable can be resisted, and the degree to which values other than those of a relentless military competition can be given their place in the attitudes and reactions of governments on both sides of the line.

POLITICS
AND THE
EAST-WEST
RELATIONSHIP

(1980)

The study of the East-West relationship has been extensively affected, and for the most part unfavorably affected, over many years by political conditions. In these opening remarks I wish to present a few thoughts about the historical development of the great tensions between the Western world and the political authority—namely, the Soviet regime—which has confronted us for more than sixty years on the other side of the ideological barrier.

This is a subject with which I have been professionally and personally involved for more than half a century. The difficulty is not that there is too little to say; rather, that there is too much. However, this problem of East-West relations is one we all have much in mind at this time in view of the special tension between the United States and the Soviet Union. It is one to which new perspectives have recently been added in the writings of Solzhenitsyn and other oppositionists or exiles from Soviet power.

When I glance back over these past fifty years, it seems evident that the East-West relationship has been burdened at all times by certain unique factors which lie in the very nature of the respective societies—factors, that is, which do not reflect just the policies of any given government at any given moment but rather deeply rooted, habitual, and in part subconscious reactions of the respective political establishments.

When it comes to describing these factors, permit me to speak—so far as the Western side is concerned—just of my own American society. Comparable things might be said, I am sure, with relation to other Western societies, but to attempt to include them in this discussion would surely take us too far.

I have no doubt that there are a number of habits, customs, and uniformities of behavior, all deeply ingrained in the American tradition, which impede, for others, the conduct of relations with the American government. There is, for example, the extensive fragmentation of authority throughout our governmental system, a fragmentation which often makes it hard for the foreign representative to know who speaks for the American government as a whole and with whom it might be useful for him to speak. There is the absence of any collective cabinet responsibility, or indeed of any system of mutual responsibility between the executive and legislative branches of government. There are the large powers exercised, even in matters that affect foreign relations, by state, local, or even private authorities with which the foreign representative cannot normally deal. There is the susceptibility of the political establishment to the emotional moods and vagaries of public opinion, particularly in this day of confusing interaction between the public and the various commercialized mass media. There is the inordinate influence exercised by individual lobbies and other organized minorities. And there is the extraordinary difficulty which such a democratic society experiences in taking a balanced view of any other country which has acquired the image of a military and political opponent or enemy—the tendency, that is, to dehumanize that image, to oversimplify it, to ignore its complexities.

In the light of these conditions, and others that might be mentioned, I can well understand that to have to deal with our government can be a frustrating experience at times for the foreign representative, the Communist representative included. I regret these circumstances, as do some other Americans. They constitute one of the reasons why I personally advocate a more modest, less ambitious American foreign policy than do many of my compatriots. But these are, I reiterate, conditions that flow from the very nature of our society, and they are not likely to be significantly changed at any early date. And I mention them only because when I go on to mention similar ones on the Soviet side, I would not like to create the impression that I view these latter as the *only* permanent impediments to a better relationship. I recognize that we Americans present a few such impediments ourselves.

But the fact is that when we look at the Soviet regime, we also encounter a whole series of customs and habits, equally deeply rooted historically, which also weigh heavily on the external relationships of that regime. These, strangely enough, seem to have been inherited much less from the models of the recent Petersburg epoch than from those of the earlier Grand Duchy of Muscovy. And they have found a remarkable reinforcement in the established traditions of Leninist Marxism itself: in its high sense of orthodoxy, its intolerance for contrary opinion, its tendency to identify ideological dissent with moral perversity, its ingrained distrust of the heretical outsider.

I might mention, as one example, the extraordinary passion for secrecy in all governmental affairs, a passion that prevents the Soviet authorities from revealing to outsiders even those aspects of their own motivation the revelation of which would be reassuring to others and would redound to their own credit. Excessive secrecy tends, after all, to invite excessive curiosity, and thus serves to provoke the very impulses against which it professes to guard.

Along with this passion for secrecy there goes a certain conspiratorial style and tradition of decision taking, particularly within the Party—a practice which may have its internal uses but often leaves others in uncertainty and inspires one degree or another of distrust. And there is also the extraordinary espionomania which appears to pervade so much of Soviet thinking. Espionage is a minor nuisance, I suppose, to most governments. But nowhere, unless it be in Albania, is the preoccupation with it so intense as it appears to be in the Soviet Union. For parallels to it, one has to turn to the Middle Ages.

And it surprises; for one would expect to encounter it, if anywhere, in a weak and precariously situated state, but not in one
of the world's greatest military powers.

However that may be, this state of mind expresses itself, of
course, in an extreme suspiciousness with relation to the individual foreigner and in the maintenance of an unusually elaborate system of supervision and control over his contacts with
Soviet citizens. The Soviet leaders, I am sure, regard this as
purely an internal matter; but it is difficult for others of us to
see it entirely this way; for relationships among individuals
across international frontiers make up a large portion of the
significant relations among states; and it seems to us that this
elaborate system of controls affects Soviet external relations,
and affects them unfortunately, in a host of ways.

These extreme tendencies, so little in accord with general
international practice, are particularly puzzling and disconcert-
ing for the outsider, because they contrast so sharply with the
correct and disarming façade of official Soviet conduct which
one often encounters when questions of internal security do
not come into play. The foreigner who has to deal with the
Soviet government often has the impression of being confronted, in rapid succession, with two quite disparate, and not
easily reconcilable, Soviet personalities: one, a correct and reasonably friendly personality which would like to see the relationship assume a normal, relaxed, and agreeable form; the
other, a personality marked by a suspiciousness so dark and
morbid, so sinister in its implications, as to constitute in itself
a form of hostility—or at least, to be explicable in no other way.
I sometimes wonder whether the Soviet leaders ever realize
how unfortunately this dual personality weighs upon the structure of the external relations of their country—how extensively
it plays into the hands of people elsewhere who are concerned
to portray the Soviet Union as a crafty, untrustworthy, and
menacing giant—how much they damage their own interests
by their cultivation of it.

Finally, there is the habit of polemic exaggeration and distortion, carried often even to the point of the denial of the
obvious and the solemn assertion of the absurd—a habit which

has offended and antagonized a host of foreigners, and to which even some of the old-timers find it hard to accustom themselves.

These, then, in both cases, are what I might call the permanent complications of the East-West relationship. They would exist, and would play their unfortunate role, in any circumstances. They place limitations on the type of peaceful coexistence that can prevail between the two worlds. They alone, however, would not preclude any peaceful coexistence at all. Unfortunately, they have not been the only major complications to which this relationship has been subject. There have been others, less permanent, but even more serious; and it is to these that we must now turn.

The first of these, and the one that marked the relationship throughout much of the 1920s and 1930s, was the world-revolutionary commitment of the early Leninist regime, with its accompanying expression in rhetoric and activity. It is true, of course, that the period of the intensive pursuit of world-revolutionary undertakings was brief. As early as 1921, aims of this nature were already ceasing to enjoy the highest priority in the policies of the Kremlin. Their place was being taken by considerations of the self-preservation of the regime and of the agricultural and industrial development of the USSR. But the world-revolutionary rhetoric remained substantially unchanged throughout the remaining years of the twenties and much of the thirties; and Moscow continued throughout that period to maintain in the various Western countries small factions of local Communist followers over whom it exerted the strictest discipline, whom it endeavored to use as instruments for the explication and pursuit of its own policies, and whose unquestioning loyalty it demanded even when this conflicted with any conceivable loyalty to their own governments. So unusual were these practices, so unprecedented in modern usage, and so disturbing to Western governments and publics, that they formed, as I then saw it and still see it in retrospect, the main cause for the high degree of tension and uncertainty then prevailing in the relations between Russia and the West.

With the triumph of Hitler in Germany, however, in the

first years of the 1930s, an important change occurred. It could not be said that the original political and ideological antagonism between Soviet Russia and the West or the offensive undertakings of the Comintern were wholly forgotten in Western circles; but beginning with 1935 the menace of Hitler began to loom larger in Western eyes than did the ideological differences with Soviet communism or the resentment of world-revolutionary activities. The result was that the Soviet Union came to be viewed in the West no longer primarily from the standpoint of its hostility to Western capitalism but rather from the standpoint of its relationship to Nazi Germany. At times this factor operated in such a way as to encourage a better and closer relationship; at other times, as in the wake of the Nazi-Soviet Non-Aggression Pact of 1939, it was just the opposite. But at all times in the years 1936 to 1946 it was the Soviet attitude towards Germany that was the decisive factor in Western attitudes towards the Soviet Union.

And this had several confusing consequences. For one thing, it tended to obscure from other attention of the Western public the full savagery and horror of the Stalinist purges of the late 1930s. But then, too, common association of the Western powers with the Soviet Union in the war against Germany gave rise to sentimental enthusiasms of one sort or another and to unreal hopes of a happy and constructive postwar collaboration with Soviet Russia. It was this factor which brought the various Western statesmen, now wholly preoccupied with the struggle against Nazi Germany, to accept without serious remonstrance, as the war came to an end, not only the recovery by the Soviet Union of those border areas of the former Russian Empire that had been lost at the time of the Revolution but also the establishment of a virtual Soviet military-political hegemony over the remainder of the eastern half of the European continent.

It was not surprising, in these circumstances, that when the Hitlerian regime had disappeared, and when people in the West turned, after the war, to the problems of the construction of a new world order, a reaction—indeed, an overreaction—set in. There was a sudden realization that the destruction of

Germany's armed power and the cession to the Soviet Union of a vast area of military deployment in the very heart of the continent had left Western Europe highly vulnerable to a Soviet military attack, or at least to heavy military-political pressures from the Soviet side. Added to this was the growing realization that with the establishment of Communist regimes, subservient to Moscow, in the various Eastern European countries, the relations of those countries with the West had become subject to the same complicating and limiting factors that already operated in relations with the Soviet Union. Then came the Korean War, a conflict in which, though Soviet forces were not actually involved, people in the West soon came to see a further manifestation of Soviet aggressiveness. And it was just at this time, of course, that the nuclear weapon began to cast its baleful shadow over the entire world scene, stirring up all those reactions of fear, confusion, and defensive panic which were bound to surround a weapon of such apocalyptic, and indeed suicidal, implications.

The death of Stalin, the establishment of the dominant position of Khrushchev, and the accompanying relaxations in Soviet policy gave rise, of course, to new hopes for the peaceful accommodation of East-West differences. Although Khrushchev was crude, he wanted, after all, no war; and he believed in human communication. But he overplayed his hand. And such favorable prospects as his influence presented went largely without response in the West. The compulsions of military competition and military thinking were already too powerful.

The Soviet leaders persisted in the traditional Russian tendency to overdo in the cultivation of military strength, particularly in conventional arms. They continued to maintain along their western borders, as their tsarist predecessors had done before them, forces numerically greater than anyone else could see the need for. For a European public already conditioned by unhappy historical experience to see the threat of military invasion behind every massing of military forces and every serious international conflict, this was enough to arouse the most lively apprehensions. And the situation was not made better by the tendency of Western strategists and military leaders to exaggerate the strength of these Soviet forces, with a view of wheedling larger military appropriations out of their own reluctant parliaments, or by the tendency of the Western press and other media to dramatize these exaggerations as a means of capturing public attention.

The Americans, meanwhile, unable to accommodate themselves to the recognition that their great country was no longer defensible, threw themselves headlong into the nuclear arms race. In the U-2 episode and the Cuban missile crisis the two great nuclear powers traded fateful mistakes, further confirming each other in the conviction that in armed force, and in armed force alone, lay their only hopes of salvation. And out of all these ingredients, including some of more recent origin, there was brewed that immensely disturbing and tragic situation in which we find ourselves today: this anxious competition in the development of new armaments; this blind dehumanization of the prospective adversary; this systematic distortion of that adversary's motivation and intentions; this steady displacement of political considerations by military ones in the calculations of statesmanship: in short, this dreadful militarization of the entire East-West relationship in concept, in rhetoric, and in assumption, which is the commanding feature—endlessly dangerous, endlessly discouraging—of this present unhappy day.

My friends: there are certain specific features of this moral and political *cul de sac* I have just described which warrant, I think, our attention on this occasion.

First: it represents a basic change, as compared with the first two decades of Soviet power, in the source of East-West tensions. Gone, or largely gone, is the world-revolutionary fervor that marked the early stages of Soviet power. Gone, too, are the anxieties that fervor provoked in Western circles. The Soviet Union is still seen as a menace, yes, but primarily as an aggressive military menace. It is not the capacity of the Kremlin for promoting social revolution in other countries that is feared and resented. Even the Soviet efforts to gain influence in the Third World are viewed primarily, not from the standpoint of their possible effects on social revolution as such, but

from the standpoint of their effects on the world balance of
military power. Were the various military anxieties to be ab-
stracted tomorrow from the contemporary scene, the Soviet
Union would still stand out on the horizons of Western statesmanship as a problem, but as a wholly different sort of problem
from that which it presented in the 1920s. There would still,
of course, be great differences and conflicts of interest. The
permanent complicating factors which I mentioned earlier on
would still be there to limit the possibilities of the relationship.
There would still remain the serious geopolitical problems presented by the abnormal Soviet positions in Eastern Europe, in
Cuba, and in Afghanistan. But Moscow would no longer figure
as the greatest inspirational source, and particularly not as the
only source, of social revolution.

Secondly, I would point out that this whole great militarization of concept about the Cold War is largely unnecessary.
There is no rational reason for it. Neither side wants a third
world war. Neither side sees in such a war a promising means
of advancing its interests. The West has no intention of attacking the Soviet Union. The Soviet leadership, I am satisfied, has
no intention, and has never had any intention, of attacking
Western Europe. The interests of the two sides conflict, to be
sure, at a number of points. Experience has proved, most unfortunately, that in smaller and more remote conflicts, where the
stakes are less than total, armed force on a limited scale might
still continue to play a certain role, whether we like it or not.
This possibility cannot, in any case, be excluded. The United
States has used its armed forces in this manner three times
since World War II: in Lebanon, in Santo Domingo, and in
Vietnam. The Soviet Union now does likewise in Afghanistan.
I am not entertaining, by these remarks, the chimera of a total
world disarmament. But for the maintenance of armed forces
on a scale that envisages the total destruction of an entire
people, not to mention the immense attendant danger to the
attacking power itself and to millions of innocent bystanders:
for this, there is no rational justification. Such a practice can
flow only from fear—sheer fear—and irrational fear at that. It
can reflect no positive aspirations.

Thirdly, while this militarization of concept and behavior is thus devoid of rational basis, it is a phenomenon of the greatest conceivable seriousness and dangerousness. It is dangerous precisely because it *needs* no rational basis—because it feeds upon itself and provides its own momentum. In fact, it commands the actions and reactions of governments to a degree greater than any positive purposes could ever achieve.

No one will understand the danger we are all in today unless he recognizes that governments in this modern world have not yet learned to cope with the compulsions that arise for them not just from an adversary's cultivation of armed force on a major scale but from their own as well. I repeat: people and governments of this present age have not yet learned how to create and cultivate great military establishments, and particularly those which include the weapons of mass destruction, without becoming the servants rather than the masters of that which they have created, and without resigning themselves helplessly to the compulsive forces they have thus unleashed.

The historical research with which I have recently been occupied has carried me back to the diplomacy of the European powers of a century ago; and I find these truths clearly evidenced in the record of those times, even though the terribleness of the weapons then at the disposal of great governments did not approach what we know today. I find instances there of great powers which had no seriously conflicting interests at all—no conflicts of interest, that is, which could remotely have justified the sacrifices and miseries of a war. Yet they, too, were carried helplessly along into the catastrophe of the First World War; and the force that carried them in that direction was simply the momentum of the weapons race in which they were then involved.

This not only *can* happen again. It *is* happening. We are all being carried along at this very moment towards a new military conflict, a conflict which could not conceivably end, for any of the parties, in anything less than disaster. It is sobering to remember that modern history offers no example of the cultivation by rival powers of armed force on a massive scale which did not in the end lead to an outbreak of hostilities.

And there is no reason to believe that our measure of control over this fateful process is any greater than that of the powers that have been caught up in it in the past. We are not greater, or wiser, than our ancestors. It would take a measure of insight, of understanding, of restraint, of willingness to accept the minor risks in order to avoid the supreme ones—it would take a measure of these qualities greater than anything yet visible on either side to permit us to release ourselves from this terrible convulsion and to save ourselves, and others, from the catastrophe to which it is leading. One is obliged to doubt that there could be any voice from within the societies of the two superpowers strong enough to bring about this act of self-emancipation, on which the future of civilization itself may depend. It would take a very strong voice, indeed a powerful chorus of voices, from the outside, to say to the decision makers of the two superpowers what should be said to them:

> "For the love of God, of your children, and of the civilization to which you belong, cease this madness. You have a duty not just to the generation of the present—you have a duty to civilization's past, which you threaten to render meaningless, and to its future, which you threaten to render nonexistent. You are mortal men. You are capable of error. You have no right to hold in your hands—there is no one wise enough and strong enough to hold in his hands—destructive powers sufficient to put an end to civilized life on a great portion of our planet. No one should wish to hold such powers. Thrust them from you. The risks you might thereby assume are not greater —could not be greater—than those which you are now incurring for us all."

This, I repeat, is what should be said to those who pursue the nuclear weapons race. But where is the voice powerful enough to say it?

There is a very special tragedy in this weapons race. It is tragic because it creates the illusion of a total conflict of interest between the two societies; and it does this at a time when their problems are in large measure really common ones. It tends to conceal the fact that both of these societies are today confronted with new internal problems which were never envisaged in either of the ideologies that originally divided them, problems that supersede the essentially nineteenth-century conditions to which both of these ideologies, and Marxism in particular, were addressed.

In part, I am referring to the environmental problems with which we are now all familiar: the question whether great industrial societies can learn to exist without polluting, exhausting, and thus destroying the natural resources essential to their very existence. These are not only problems common to the two ideological worlds; they are ones for the solution of which they require each other's collaboration, not each other's enmity.

But beyond that, there are deeper problems—social and even moral and spiritual—which are coming increasingly to affect all the highly industrialized, urbanized, and technologically advanced societies of this modern age. What is involved here is essentially the question as to how life is to be given an adequate meaning, how the quality of life and experience is to be assured, for the individual citizen in the highly artificial and overcomplicated social environment that modern technology has created. Neither of us, neither we in the West nor they in the East, is doing too well in the solution of these problems. Neither of us has much to be proud about. We are both failing, each in his own way. If one wants an example of this, one has only to glance at the condition of youth on both sides of the line. The Russians demoralize their young people by giving them too little freedom. We demoralize ours by giving them too much. Neither system finds itself able to give them what they need in the way of leadership and inspiration and guidance if they are to realize their own potentialities as individuals and to meet the responsibilities which the future is inevitably going to place upon them.

And this is only one of the points at which we are failing. Neither here nor there is the direction society is taking really under control. We are all being swept along, in our fatuous pride, by currents which we do not understand and over which we have no command. And we will not protect ourselves from the resulting dangers by continuing to pour great portions of our substance, year after year, into the instruments of military destruction. On the contrary, we will only be depriving ourselves, by this prodigality, of the resources essential for any hopeful attack on these profound emerging problems.

The present moment is in many respects a crucial one. Not for thirty years has the political tension reached so high and dangerous a point as it has today. Not in all this time has there been so high a degree of misunderstanding, of suspicion, of bewilderment, and of sheer military fear.

We must expect that in both the Soviet Union and the United States the coming months will see extensive changes in governmental leadership. Will the new leaders be able to reverse these trends?

It will not be too late for them to make the effort to do so. There are limits, of course, to what one could hope to achieve. The permanent impediments to a happier relationship, which I outlined at the outset of this address, would still be there and would not be rapidly overcome, even in the best of circumstances. But this would not preclude, in fact, the attainment of a real turning point beyond which anxiety and pessimism would begin to be replaced by hope and confidence for people everywhere.

Two things, as I see it, would be necessary to make possible this sort of transition.

First, of course, would be the overcoming of the military fixations that now command in so high degree the reactions on both sides, and the mustering of greater courage by the statesmen in facing up to the task of relating military affairs to the other needs of the state. What is urgently needed is that statesmen on both sides of the line should take their military establishments in hand and insist that these should become the servants, not the masters and determinants, of political action. On both sides, one must learn to accept the fact that there is no security to be found in the quest for military superiority; that only in the reduction, not the multiplication, of the existing monstrous arsenals can the true security of any nation be found.

But beyond this, when it comes to the more normal and permanent problems of foreign policy, both of the superpowers could serve the cause of peace by developing a bit more humility in their view of themselves and of their relationship to their world environment, particularly the Third World. Both could take better account of the bitterness of their own domestic problems, and of the need for overcoming some of these problems before indulging themselves in dreams of external grandeur and world leadership. Only by overcoming these glaring domestic deficiencies can they improve their capacity for being helpful, or even impressive, to the world around them. Only by improving their quality as models can they make credible a claim to world leadership.

If we, the scholars, with our patient and unsensational labors, can help the statesmen to understand these basic truths —if we can help them to understand not only the dangers we face and the responsibility they bear for overcoming these dangers but also the constructive and hopeful possibilities that lie there to be opened up by wiser, more restrained, and more realistic policies—if we can do these things, then we will be richly repaid for our dedication and our persistence; for we will then have the satisfaction of knowing that scholarship, the highest work of the mind, has served, as it should, the highest interests of civilization. (Speech delivered in Garmisch, Germany, before the Second World Congress on Soviet and East European Studies, 10/1/80.)

A RISKY
EQUATION

(1981)
*"Take but degree away, untune that string
And, hark! what discord follows. . . ."*

—*Troilus and Cressida*

These deeply perceptive words by Shakespeare have their relevance to a sizable section of United States opinion, official and private, on the Soviet Union.

It is not that there is no truth in many of the things that people say and believe about the Russians; it is rather that what they say and believe involves a great deal of exaggeration and oversimplification. And this is serious, because there are times when exaggeration and oversimplification, being harder than falsehood to spot, can be fully as pernicious.

We are told that the official Soviet outlook is one of total cynicism and power-hungry opportunism. Is this view wrong? Not entirely. But it is overdrawn. The way in which the outlooks of the present Soviet leaders, tempered as these outlooks are by the discipline of long political experience and responsibility, relate to the sanguine ruthlessness of the pure Leninist doctrine as conceived some sixty years ago in the heat of the revolutionary struggle is complicated. There is traditional lip service to established doctrine; there is also considerable inner detachment.

The Soviet leadership, we are told, is fanatically devoted to the early achievement of world revolution. Is this allegation wrong? Partly, and it is certainly misleading. It ignores the dis-

tinction between what Soviet Communists think would be ideal-
ly desirable and what they see as necessary or possible to try to
achieve at the present moment. It also ignores the distinction
between what they claim they believe will ultimately occur and
what they actually intend to bring about by their own actions.

We hear much about the menacing scale of Soviet military
programs and the resulting tilting of the arms balance in our
disfavor. Wrong? Again, not entirely, but often exaggerated.
Part of this view rests on "worst-case" calculations, particularly
regarding conventional armaments. Often, it ignores our own
contribution to the adversely developing balance—by our unrestrained inflation and by the various unnecessary deficiencies of
our conventional forces. Much of it is corrupted by the fundamental error of measuring armaments, weapon for weapon,
against another country's armaments instead of against one's
own needs, as though the needs of any two great countries were
identical and any statistical disparity between their arsenals was
a mark of somebody's superiority or inferiority.

We hear of the menace of Soviet expansionism or "adven-
tures" in the Third World. Is this all wrong? No, not all. The
Soviet presence in Cuba, in which we should never have tacitly
acquiesced in the first place, is not indefinitely compatible with
our vital interests. Soviet collaboration with, and support for,
Colonel Muammar el-Qaddafi, the Libyan leader, is a signal
disservice to the stability of the Near East. The occupation of
Afghanistan has created serious international complications.
Yet in general, such Soviet efforts have not been very successful. The Soviet Union's position in the Third World is actually
weaker than it was years ago, before the disruption of Moscow's
relationships with Peking, Cairo, and Jakarta. And the methods by which Moscow recently has been trying to gain influence in the Third World, primarily the dispatch of arms and
military advisers, resemble too closely our own for us to indulge
gracefully in transports of moral indignation.

It is alleged that the Soviet leaders never respect international agreements. Right? Mainly not. Their record in the
fulfillment of clear and specific written obligations, especially
those that avoid questions of motivation and simply state precisely what each side will do and when, has not been bad at all.

Vague assurances of high-minded general purpose, on the other hand, such as those embedded in the Helsinki agreements, are viewed by them with the same cynicism they attribute to the other party who signs such documents.

It is asserted that no useful collaboration with the Soviet Union is possible. True? Not really. There is indeed an extensive area within which what we would consider normal and intimate relations are not possible, their being precluded by Soviet ideological commitments, procedural habits, and other oddities, not to mention a few of our own. But there is another area, admittedly limited, involving certain forms of travel, trade, scholarly exchange, and collaboration in cultural and other nonpolitical fields, where things are different. And it is important that this area not be neglected, for interaction of this sort, in addition to increasing our knowledge and understanding of Soviet society, serves as an indispensable cushion, absorbing some of the shock of the misunderstandings and conflicts that may occur in other fields.

In a relationship of such immense importance as the Soviet-American one, there should be no room for such extremisms and oversimplifications. Not only do they produce their counterparts on the other side, but they confuse us. They cause us to see as totally unsolvable a problem that is only partly so.

Soviet society is made up of human beings like ourselves. Because it is human, it is complex. It is not, as many of the oversimplifications would suggest, a static, unchanging phenomenon. It too evolves, and the direction in which it evolves is influenced to some degree by our vision of it and our treatment of it.

What is needed on our part is not an effort to prove our own virtue by dramatizing Soviet iniquities, but rather a serious effort to study Soviet society in all its complexity and to form realistic, sophisticated judgments about the nature and dimensions of the problem it presents for us. If we do this, there is no reason to suppose that the conflicts of interest that divide these two great countries, so different in geography, in history, and in tradition, should lead to the sort of disastrous climax that modern weapons, most tragically, now make possible.
(*New York Times* Op-Ed article, 2/18/81.)

10

TWO VIEWS OF THE SOVIET PROBLEM

(1981)

Looking back over the whole course of the differences between my own view of East-West relations and those of my various critics and opponents in recent years, I have to conclude that the differences have been, essentially, not ones of interpretation of phenomena about the reality of which we all agree but, rather, differences over the nature and significance of the observable phenomena themselves: in other words, differences not about the meaning of what we see but, rather, about what it is that we see in the first place.

Let me illustrate this first with the example of our differing views of the nature of the Soviet regime itself.

My opponents, if I do not misinterpret their position, see the Soviet leaders as a group of men animated primarily by a desire to achieve further expansion of their effective power, and this at the expense of the independence and the liberties of other people—at the expense of the stability, if not the peace, of international life. They see these men as pursuing a reckless and gigantic buildup of their own armed forces, a buildup of such dimensions that it cannot be explained by defensive considerations alone and must therefore, it is reasoned, reflect aggressive ones. They see them as eager to bring other countries, in the Third World and elsewwhere, under their domination, in order to use those countries as pawns against the United States and other nations of the Western

alliance; and they see the situations existing today in such
places as Angola and Ethiopia and Afghanistan as examples of
the dangerous success of these endeavors. My opponents reject
the suggestion that Soviet policy might be motivated in any
important degree by defensive considerations. In their view,
the Soviet leaders do not feel politically encircled or in any
other way significantly threatened. And though it is recognized
that Moscow faces serious internal problems, it is not thought
that these problems impose any very serious limitations on the
freedom of the regime to pursue aggressive external intentions.
What emerges from this vision is, of course, an image of the
Soviet regime not greatly different from the image of the Nazi
regime as it existed shortly before the outbreak of the Second
World War. This being the case, it is not surprising that the
conclusion should be drawn that the main task for Western
statesmanship at this time must be to avoid what are now
generally regarded as the great mistakes of the Western powers
in the late 1930s: that is, to avoid what is called appeasement,
to give a low priority to the possibilities for negotiation and
accommodation, and to concentrate on the building up of a
military posture so imposing and forbidding, and a Western
unity so unshakable, that the Soviet leaders will perceive the
futility and the danger of their aggressive plans, and will accept
the necessity of learning to live side by side with other nations
on a basis compatible with the security of those other nations
and with the general requirements of world stability and peace.
I do not question the good faith of American governmental
personalities when they say that once this new relationship of
military and political power has been established, they will be
prepared to sit down with their Soviet counterparts and discuss
with them the prerequisites for a safer world; but I fear that
they see the success of any such discussions as something to
which the Soviet leaders could be brought only reluctantly,
with gnashing of teeth, and this seems to me to be a poor
augury for the lasting quality of any results that might be
achieved.

Now, all this, as I say, is what I believe my opponents see
when they turn their eyes in the direction of the Kremlin.

What I see is something quite different. I see a group of troubled men—elderly men, for the most part—whose choices and possibilities are severely constrained. I see these men as the prisoners of many circumstances: prisoners of their own past and their country's past; prisoners of the antiquated ideology to which their extreme sense of orthodoxy binds them; prisoners of the rigid system of power that has given them their authority; but prisoners, too, of certain ingrained peculiarities of the Russian statesmanship of earlier ages—the congenital sense of insecurity, the lack of inner self-confidence, the distrust of the foreigner and the foreigner's world, the passion for secrecy, the neurotic fear of penetration by other powers into areas close to their borders, and a persistent tendency, resulting from all these other factors, to overdo the creation of military strength. I see here men deeply preoccupied, as were their tsarist Russian predecessors, with questions of prestige—preoccupied more, in many instances, with the appearances than with the realities. I do not see them as men anxious to expand their power by the direct use of their armed forces, although they could easily be frightened into efforts that would have this appearance. I see them as indeed concerned—and rather naturally concerned—to increase their influence among Third World countries. This neither surprises me nor alarms me. Most great powers have similar desires. And the methods adopted by the Soviet Union are not very different from those adopted by some of the others. Besides, what has distinguished these Soviet efforts, historically viewed, seems to be not their success but precisely their lack of it. I see no recent Soviet achievements in this direction which would remotely outweigh the great failures of the postwar period: in Yugoslavia, in China, and in Egypt.

But, beyond that, a wish to expand one's *influence* is not the same thing as a wish to expand the formal limits of one's power and responsibility. This I do not think the Soviet leaders at all wish to do. Specifically, I have seen no evidence of any disposition on their part to invade Western Europe and thus to take any further parts of it formally under their authority. They are having trouble enough with the responsibilities they have already undertaken in Eastern Europe. They have no reason to wish to increase these burdens. I can conceive that there might be certain European regions, outside the limits of their present hegemony, where they would be happy, for defensive reasons, to have some sort of military control, if such control could be acquired safely and easily without too much disruption of international stability; but it is a far cry from this to the assumption that they would be disposed to invade any of these areas out of the blue, in peacetime, at the cost of unleashing another world war.

It is my belief that these men do indeed consider the Soviet Union to have been increasingly isolated and in danger of encirclement by hostile powers in recent years. I do not see how they could otherwise interpret the American military relationship with Iran in the time of the shah or the more recent American military relationships with Pakistan and China. And these, I believe, are not the only considerations that would limit the freedom of the Soviet leaders to indulge themselves in dreams of external expansion, even if they were inclined towards such dreams. They are obviously very conscious of the dangers of a disintegration of their dominant position in Eastern Europe, and particularly in Poland; and this not because they have any conscious desire to mistreat or oppress the peoples involved but because they see any further deterioration of the situation there as a threat to their political and strategic interests in Germany—interests that are unquestionably highly defensive in origin.

I believe, too, that internal developments in the Soviet Union also present a heavy claim on the attention and the priorities of the Soviet leaders. They are deeply committed to the completion of their existing programs for the economic and social development of the Soviet peoples; and I am sure that they are very seriously concerned over the numerous problems that have recently been impeding that completion: the perennial agricultural failures; the many signs of public apathy, demoralization, drunkenness, and labor absenteeism; the imbalance in population growth between the Russian center and the non-Russian periphery; the growing shortage of skilled labor; and the widespread economic corruption and indiscipline.

They may differ among themselves as to how these problems should be approached, but I doubt that there are any of them who think that the problems could be solved by the unleashing of another world war. I emphatically reject the primitive thesis, drawn largely from misleading and outdated nineteenth-century examples, that the Kremlin might be inclined to resort to war as a means of resolving its internal difficulties. Nothing in Russian history or psychology supports such a thesis.

In saying these things, I do not mean to deny that there exist, interwoven with the rest of the pattern of Soviet diplomacy, certain disquieting tendencies, which oblige Western policymakers to exercise a sharp vigilance even as they pursue their efforts towards peace. I believe that these tendencies reflect not so much any thirst for direct aggression as an over-suspiciousness, a fear of being tricked or outsmarted, an exaggerated sense of prestige, and an interpretation of Russia's defensive needs so extreme—so extravagant and so far-reaching—that it becomes in itself a threat, or an apparent threat, to the security of other nations. While these weaknesses probably affect all Soviet statesmen to one extent or another, the evidence suggests to me that they are concentrated particularly in specific elements of the Soviet power structure—notably, in the military and naval commands, in the vast police establishment, and in certain sections of the Party apparatus. So far, these tendencies do not seem to me to have dominated Soviet policy, except in the case of the decision to intervene in Afghanistan—a decision that was taken in somewhat abnormal circumstances and is now, I believe, largely recognized, even in Moscow, as a mistake. But there will soon have to be extensive changes in the occupancy of the senior political positions in Moscow, and Western policymakers should consider that a Western policy that offers no encouragement to the more moderate elements in the Soviet hierarchy must inevitably strengthen the hand, and the political position, of those who are not moderate at all.

So much, then, for our differences of view with respect to the Soviet regime. It is not unnatural that anyone who sees the phenomenon of Soviet power so differently from certain others should also differ from those others in his view of the best response to it. It is clear that my opponents see the Soviet regime primarily as a great, immediate, and growing military danger, and that this conditions their idea of the best response. I have no argument with them about the existence of a great danger. I do differ from them with regard to the *causes* of this danger. I see these causes not in the supposed "aggressiveness" of either side but in the weapons race itself. I see it in the compulsions that this, like any other weapons race between sovereign powers, engenders within all the participating parties. I see it in the terrible militarization of outlook to which this sort of competition conduces: a species of obsession which causes those who have succumbed to it to direct their vision and their efforts exclusively to the hopeless contingencies of military conflict, to ignore the more hopeful ones of communication and accommodation, and in this way to enhance the very dangers against which they fancy themselves to be working.

Leaving aside for the moment the problems of nuclear weaponry, I shall say a word about the military balance in conventional weapons. An impression has been created that there has recently been a new and vast buildup of Soviet conventional strength on the European continent, changing the balance of forces in this respect strongly to the disadvantage of the West. This view has found expression in the statements of a number of distinguished Western personalities. I cannot flatly deny the correctness of this thesis. I am only a private citizen. I do not have access to all the information at the disposition of the governments. But, with all respect for the sincerity and good faith of those who advance this view, I am disinclined to accept it just on the basis of their say-so. I am so disinclined because I think I have made a reasonable effort, in these last few years, to follow such information as appears in the press and the other media about the military balance, and I find this body of information confused, contradictory, statistically questionable, and often misleading. Most of it appears to derive from data leaked to the media by one or another of the Western military-intelligence services, and one cannot avoid the impression that it reflects a tendency to paint an exaggerated and frightening picture of Soviet capacities and intentions—a so-called worst-case image. This is done, no doubt, partly out of an excessive professional prudence but partly, too, I am afraid, with an eye to the reactions of various Western parliamentary bodies, which require to be frightened (or so it is believed) before they will make reasonable appropriations for defense. I can only say that if the NATO governments really wish us, the public, to believe in the reality of a recent dramatic increase in the Soviet conventional threat to Western Europe, they will have to place before us a more consistent and plausible statistical basis for that view than anything they have given us to date. In terms neither of the number of divisions nor of total manpower nor of any of the other major indicators does the information now available to the ordinary newspaper reader prove that the balance of conventional military strength in Central Europe is significantly less favorable to the Western side than it was ten or twenty years ago.

To say this is not to claim that the present balance is satisfactory. That is not my contention. Of course there is a preponderance of strength on the Soviet side. Such a preponderance has existed since the Second World War. Of course it is not desirable. I myself favor a strengthening of NATO's conventional capacities, particularly if the strengthening be taken to mean an improvement of morale, of discipline, of training and alertness, and not just a heaping up of fancy and expensive new equipment that we do not have the manpower to operate or the money to maintain. But if this strengthening is to be effected, I think it should be presented and defended to the public as a normal policy of prudence, a reasonable long-term precaution in a troubled time, and not as something responding to any specific threat from any specific quarter. The Western governments, in particular, should not try to gain support for such a program by painting on the wall an exaggerated and unnecessarily alarming image of Soviet intentions and capacities. This procedure represents, in my view, an abuse of public confidence, and one that, in the end, is invariably revenged.

So much for the conventional weapons. Now—with a sigh

and a sinking of the heart—for the nuclear ones. Here, I am sorry to say, I have differences with every single one of the premises on which our government, and some of the other NATO governments, seem to act in designing their policies in this field. First of all, my opponents seem to see the nuclear explosive as just a weapon like any other weapon, only more destructive; and they think that because it is more destructive it is a better and more powerful weapon. I deny that the nuclear explosive is a proper weapon. It conforms, in my view, to none of the criteria traditionally applied to conventional weapons. It can serve no useful purpose. It cannot be used without bringing disaster upon everyone concerned. I regard it as the reflection of a vast misunderstanding of the true purposes of warfare and the true usefulness of weaponry.

My opponents see the Soviet Union as having sought and achieved some sort of statistical superiority over the NATO powers in this kind of weaponry. I myself have not seen the evidence that it has achieved that sort of superiority; nor do I see any reason to assume that that is what it would like to do. The evidence seems to me to suggest that it is striving for what it would view as equivalence, in the statistical sense—not for superiority. My opponents believe that differences of superority or inferiority, in the statistical sense, have meaning: that if you have more of these weapons than your adversary has, you are in a stronger position to stand up against intimidation or against an actual attack. I challenge that view. I submit that if you are talking, as all of us are talking today, about what are in reality grotesque quanties of overkill—arsenals so excessive that they would suffice to destroy the adversary's homeland many times over—statistical disparities between the arsenals on the two sides are quite meaningless. But precisely that—the absurd excessiveness of the existing nuclear arsenals—is the situation we have before us.

My opponents maintain that we must have the nuclear weapons, because in a conflict we would not be able to match the Soviet Union with the conventional ones. I would say: If this is true, let us correct the situation at once. Neither with respect to manpower nor with respect to industrial potential are we lacking in the means to put up conventional forces fully as strong as those deployed against us in Europe. My opponents say: We must have these weapons for purposes of deterrence. The use of this term carries two implications: first, that it is the Russians who have taken the lead in the development of these weapons, and that we are only reacting to what they have done; and, secondly, that the Russians are such monsters that unless they are deterred they would assuredly launch upon us a nuclear attack, with all the horrors and sufferings that that would bring. I question both these implications; and I question in particular the wisdom of suggesting the latter implication thousands of times a year to the general public, thus schooling the public mind to believe that our Soviet adversary has lost every semblance of humanity and is concerned only to wreak unlimited destruction for destruction's sake. I am not sure, furthermore, that the stationing of these weapons on one's territory is not more of a provocation of their use by others than a means of dissuading others from using them. I have never been an advocate of unilateral disarmament; and I see no necessity for anything of that sort today. But I must say that if we Americans had no nuclear weapons whatsoever on our soil instead of the tens of thousands of nuclear warheads we are now said to have deployed, I would feel the future of my children and grandchildren to be far safer than I do at this moment; for if there is any incentive for the Russians to use such weapons against us, it surely comes in overwhelming degree—probably, in fact, entirely—from our own enormous deployment of them.

Finally, there are many people who consider it useless, or even undesirable, to try to get rid of these weapons entirely, and believe that a satisfactory solution can somehow be found by halfway measures of one sort or another—agreements that would limit their numbers or their destructiveness or the areas of their deployment. Such speculations come particularly easily to a government such as our own, which has long regarded nuclear weapons as essential to its defensive posture and has not been willing to contemplate a future without them. I have no confidence in any of these schemes. I see the danger, not in the number or quality of the weapons or in the intentions of those who hold them, but in the very existence of weapons of this nature, regardless of whose hands they are in. I believe that until we consent to recognize that the nuclear weapons we hold in our own hands are as much a danger to us as those that repose in the hands of our supposed adversaries, there will be no escape from the confusions and dilemmas to which such weapons have now brought us, and must bring us increasingly as time goes on. For this reason, I see no solution to the problem other than the complete elimination of these and all other weapons of mass destruction from national arsenals; and the sooner we move towards that solution, and the greater courage we show in doing so, the safer we will be. (Speech delivered to the P.E.N Club, Oslo, Norway, 8/14/81.)

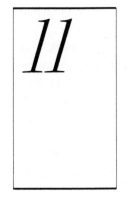

11

AFGHANISTAN AND POLAND

AFGHANISTAN
(1980)

The Soviet Occupation

On Christmas Day 1979, after more than a century of periodic involvement with the internal affairs of its turbulent neighbor, and after many months of futile effort to find a pro-Soviet Afghan figure capable of running the country, the Soviet government suddenly expanded what was already a sizable military involvement in Afghanistan into a full-fledged occupation, promising that the troops would leave when their limited mission had been accomplished.

This move was not only abrupt—no effort had been made to prepare world opinion for it—but it was executed with incredible political clumsiness. The pretext offered was an insult to the intelligence of even the most credulous of Moscow's followers. The world community was left with no alternative but to condemn the operation in the strongest terms, and it has done so.

So bizarre was the Soviet action that one is moved to wonder whence exactly, in the closely shielded recesses of Soviet policy-making, came the inspiration for it and the political influence

to achieve its approval. It was a move decidedly not in character for either Aleksei N. Kosygin or Leonid I. Brezhnev. (The
one was, of course, ill and removed from active work. The
limitations on the other's health and powers of attention are
well known.) Andrei A. Gromyko, too, is unlikely to have
approved it. These reflections suggest the recent breakthrough,
to positions of dominant influence, of hard-line elements much
less concerned for world opinion, but also much less experienced than these older figures.

Such a change was not unexpected by the more attentive
Kremlinologists, particularly in the light of the recent deterioration of Soviet-American relations, but it was assumed that it
would take place only in connection with, and coincidental
with, the retirement of Mr. Brezhnev and other older Politburo
members. That it could occur with the preservation of Mr.
Brezhnev as a figurehead was not foreseen.

Be that as it may, this ill-considered move was bound to be
unacceptable to the world community, and the United States
had no alternative but to join in the condemnation of it in the
United Nations. But beyond that point, the American official
reaction has revealed a disquieting lack of balance, both in the
analysis of the problem and then, not surprisingly, in the response to it.

In the official American interpretation of what occurred in
Afghanistan, no serious account appears to have been taken of
such specific factors as geographic proximity, ethnic affinity of
peoples on both sides of the border, and political instability in
what is, after all, a border country of the Soviet Union. Now,
specific factors of this nature, all suggesting defensive rather
than offensive impulses, may not have been all there was to
Soviet motivation, nor would they have sufficed to justify the
action; but they were relevant to it and should have been given
their due in any realistic appraisal of it.

Instead of this, the American view of the Soviet action
appears to have run overwhelmingly to the assumption that it
was a prelude to aggressive military moves against various countries and regions further afield. No one can guarantee, of
course, that one or another such move will not take place. A

war atmosphere has been created. Discussion in Washington has been dominated by talk of American military responses— of the acquisition of bases and facilities, of the creation of a rapid-deployment force, of the cultivation of military ties with other countries all along Russia's sensitive southern border. In these circumstances, anything can happen. But the fact is, this extravagant view of Soviet motivation rests, to date, exclusively on our own assumptions. I am not aware of any substantiation of it in anything the Soviet leaders themselves have said or done. On the contrary, Mr. Brezhnev has specifically, publicly, and vigorously denied any such intentions.

In the light of these assumptions we have been prodigal with strident public warnings to the Russians, some of them issued even prior to the occupation of Afghanistan, not to attack this place or that, assuring them that if they did so, we would respond by military means. Can this really be sound procedure? Warnings of this nature are implicit accusations as well as commitments. We are speaking here of a neighboring area of the Soviet Union, not of the United States. Aside from the question whether we could really back up these pronouncements if our hand were to be called, is it really wise—is it not in fact a practice pregnant with possibilities for resentment and for misreading of signals—to go warning people publicly not to do things they have never evinced any intention of doing?

This distortion in our assessment of the Soviet motivation has affected, not unnaturally, our view of other factors in the Middle Eastern situation. What else but a serious lack of balance could explain our readiness to forget, in the case of Pakistan, the insecurity of the present government, its recent callous jeopardizing of the lives of our embassy personnel, its lack of candor about its nuclear programs—and then to invite humiliation by pressing upon it offers of military aid that elicited only insult and contempt? What else could explain, in the case of Iran, our sudden readiness—if only the hostages were released—to forget not only their sufferings but all the flag-burnings, the threatening fists, the hate-ridden faces, and the cries of "Death to Carter," and to offer to take these very people to our bosom in a common resistance to Soviet aggressiveness? What else could explain our naïve hope that the Arab states could be induced, just by the shock of Afghanistan, to forget their differences with Israel and to join us in an effort to contain the supposedly power-mad Russians?

This last merits a special word. I have already referred to the war atmosphere in Washington. Never since World War II has there been so far-reaching a militarization of thought and discourse in the capital. An unsuspecting stranger, plunged into its midst, could only conclude that the last hope of peaceful, nonmilitary solutions had been exhausted—that from now on only weapons, however used, could count.

These words are not meant to express opposition to a prompt and effective strengthening of our military capabilities relevant to the Middle East. If what was involved here was the carrying of a big stick while speaking softly rather than the carrying of a relatively small stick while thundering all over the place, who could object? But do we not, by this preoccupation with a Soviet military threat, the reality of which remains to be proved, run the risk of forgetting that the greatest real threats to our security in that region remain what they have been all along: our self-created dependence on Arab oil and our involvement in a wholly unstable Israeli-Arab relationship, neither of which is susceptible of correction by purely military means, and in neither of which is the Soviet Union the major factor?

If the Persian Gulf is really vital to our security, it is surely we who, by our unrestrained greed for oil, have made it so. Would it not be better to set about to eliminate, by a really serious and determined effort, a dependence that ought never have been allowed to arise, than to try to shore up by military means, in a highly unfavorable region, the unsound position into which the dependence has led us? Military force might conceivably become necessary as a supplement to such an effort; it could never be an adequate substitute for it.

The oddest expression of this lack of balance is perhaps in the bilateral measures with which we conceive ourselves to have punished the Russian action. Aside from the fact that it is an open question whom we punished most by these measures —Russia or ourselves—we have portrayed them as illustrations of what could happen to Moscow if it proceeded to one or another of the future aggresive acts we credit it with plotting.

But that is precisely what these measures are not; for they represent cards that have already been played and cannot be played twice. There was never any reason to suppose that the Soviet government, its prestige once engaged, could be brought by open pressure of this nature to withdraw its troops from Afghanistan. But this means, then, that we have expended, for what was really a hopeless purpose, all the important nonmilitary cards we conceived ourselves as holding in our hands. Barring a resort to war, the Soviet government has already absorbed the worst of what we have to offer, and has nothing further to fear from us. Was this really mature statesmanship on our part?

We are now in the danger zone. I can think of no instance in modern history where such a breakdown of political communication and such a triumph of unrestrained military suspicion as now marks Soviet-American relations has not led, in the end, to armed conflict. The danger is heightened by the fact that we do not know, at this time, with whom we really have to deal at the Soviet end. If there was ever a time for realism, prudence, and restraint in American statesmanship, it is this one. Nothing in the passions of electoral politics could serve as the slightest excuse for ignoring this necessity. (*New York Times* Op-Ed article, 2/1/80.)

The Stabilization of the Situation

What is needed here, from our standpoint, is not a total renunciation by the Soviet government of its political interest in Afghanistan. It is, after all, a border country of the Soviet Union. Its internal life has long been marked by periodic instability. Moscow is understandably sensitive to anything that smacks of penetration and intrigue in this region by other major powers.

What *is* needed, from our standpoint, is the gradual dismantling of the present Soviet military involvement and the establishment there of something resembling a genuine native regime, of whatever complexion. Such a development is not apt to be promoted by open pressure from ourselves: by ultimata or demands, that is, that merely put the Soviet government on the spot and engage its prestige. It is not apt to be promoted by our cultivation of military relationships with others of Russia's southern neighbors, particularly the Chinese, which give the impression of an effort at military domination of the entire region by a United States–inspired military alliance. It may well be that civil resistance to the Soviet occupation among the native population will grow to such a level that the Soviet leaders will conclude that the effort to pacify the country and to hold it in subjection is not worth the candle, and will seek ways to withdraw at minimal damage to their own interests and prestige. But this will not be easy for them to do if it appears that the resistance in question is one extensively inspired and supported by foreign powers, particularly China and the United States. If this should be the prevailing impression in world opinion at the time in question, then Moscow might feel itself compelled to hang on even though it would like, on principle, to withdraw—to hang on, that is, at least to the cities, airports, and major highways. And I know of no reason to suppose that it could not succeed in doing this for a long time, if no more acceptable alternative were visible.

The foregoing has not taken account of the much-discussed contingency of some further Soviet military move in the Middle Eastern region. I have personally seen nothing in Soviet statements or behavior to suggest that the Soviet leaders are contemplating any such move. In the case of Pakistan, in particular, anything of that sort (unless it were a very limited action to eliminate Afghan guerrilla sanctuaries on the Pakistan side of the border) seems most unlikely. But in a highly militarized situation such as we have before us today, and in view of the uncertain situation now prevailing within the Soviet leadership, no eventualities can be entirely ruled out.

Should anything of this sort occur, our response would have to be governed by the nature and apparent purpose of the action in question. Certain conceivable actions of this sort would presumably engage our vital interests; others would not necessarily do so.

I would not like to be thought of, in any case, as being

opposed to the strengthening of American military capabilities relevant to the problems of that region. There are several contingencies in which the use of American military force might, in my view, prove justifiable and unavoidable. Unless and until such contingencies arise, however, I think it of highest importance that whatever strengthening we give to our forces be done quietly and unprovocatively, and that the greatest care be taken to see that it is presented to our public and to the world public as a reasonable and restrained precaution, and not as an indication that we regard armed conflict as inevitable, that we are placing all our attention and all our hopes on the military card, or that we have effectively abandoned serious efforts to arrive at nonmilitary solutions to the problems of the region. This, I regret to say, seems to me to be the impression that has been conveyed by much of the recent discussion of these problems in our press and other media, as well as by certain statements by governmental officials, not to mention the extraordinary abundance of deliberate anonymous leaks on military matters from military and intelligence sources within our government. There will, as I see it, have to be considerably more restraint in official public utterance, and a much greater discipline exerted over the leaking of military information from various sources within the government, before we can truly say that we have done all in our power to prevent the present situation in the Gulf region from degenerating into forms of conflict that could only end disastrously for all concerned.

POLAND
(1982)

Jaruzelski's Course

The Soviet hegemony established in Eastern Europe in 1945 was from the start an unnatural—and, in the long run, untenable—arrangement.

This hegemony was bound to yield, with the passage of time,

to a state of affairs more compatible with geopolitical realities, including the traditions and feelings of the affected
peoples, and their capacities for leading a successful independent national existence. The question was only how, at
what pace, and in what manner the change would come
about.

That this change could proceed peacefully and successfully,
provided that the process was gradual and did not pose too
sharp a challenge to the perceived security interests of an
inwardly insecure Soviet regime, has been demonstrated by
numerous developments of the past quarter of a century, and
nowhere more strikingly than in Poland itself.

Had Solidarity been willing to pause as recently as a month
or two ago—to rest for a while on its laurels and to give time
for Moscow to satisfy itself that freedom in Poland did not
mean the immediate collapse of the heavens—it would already
have had to its credit a historic achievement in the way of
national self-liberation, one that far exceeded anything seen in
Eastern Europe since the Yugoslav break in 1948. It would
have been essential, of course, that Poland's continued mem-
bership in the Warsaw Pact and its retention of a "socialist"
(whatever that means) form of government not be challenged.
But this, of course, was not the road that Solidarity, or at least
a part of Solidarity, took.

What has now occurred is bad—of course. But it could be
worse. General Wojciech Jaruzelski has given his assurance
that if and when public order is restored, martial law will be
removed and democratic reforms instituted. This is, actually,
a course almost dictated by circumstances. General Jaruzelski
is, after all, a Pole, surrounded by Poles, and a return to the old
order is unthinkable. How successful he will be in this undertaking remains to be seen. Something, certainly, will depend
upon the extent to which he is able to restrain the more
aggressive members of his own army and police and to prevent
the sort of brutalities already rumored to have taken place. But
perhaps it is best that he should be given a chance to show what
he can do.

A return to the combination of a semiparalyzed Communist
government and a Solidarity well set up to obstruct this govern-

ment, but in no way prepared to replace it, was not the ideal solution for Poland either.

It was, after all, under just that sort of confusion of responsibilities that Poland's economic and financial position declined disastrously during the past year. A return to all this now would also promise something decidedly less than an ideal situation. Such a reversion would wholly demoralize the army and the governmental apparatus, such as it is, without providing anything to replace it. It is questionable how effective it would be in assuring vigorous and regular economic activity— and this is a vital point, for if there was ever an urgent need for people to work, and to work hard, if they expect to eat, it is in Poland today. So serious is the financial and economic plight of Poland that restoration of industrial and agricultural productivity should be recognized, for the moment, as the supreme necessity of Polish public life. Other things can better wait.

Finally, and most important of all, a return to the *status quo ante* would strain to the breaking point that modicum of patience that has, after all, thus far kept the Soviet leadership from intervening directly with its own forces.

The sanctions imposed on the Polish government by the Reagan administration are now a *fait accompli.* They have documented our sympathies, if they have done little else. They must presumably be maintained, at least for some time.

Perhaps it is fortunate that these sanctions are not more effective than they are, for this means that there is still time for our government to do what it might better have done from the outset: namely, to reserve judgment in the face of a rapidly moving and unpredictable situation that we have little capability of influencing in any case, to keep its own counsel for a time, to stop needling our allies, and to wait until a few more of the returns are in before considering what, if anything, we might usefully do. (*New York Times* Op-Ed article, 1/5/82.)

As the Kremlin Sees It

The sanctions imposed on the Soviet Union by the Reagan administration are, unfortunately, marked by an extreme

vagueness about what the Soviet regime would be expected to
do to bring about their removal.

One is reluctant to believe that what is wanted is that
Moscow should order the government in Warsaw to undo what
has been done since December 13, and to resotre the *status quo
ante,* because such exertion of authority by Moscow over Warsaw is precisely what we profess to deplore.

One can only assume that what is wanted is that the Soviet
government should take a detached attitude towards events in
Poland and permit the sitaution there to find its own level,
whatever the consequences for Poland's form of government
or that country's international position.

This, however, would be a drastic demand. It would reach
to the very foundation of the de facto division of Europe that
has existed since World War II. This division itself was a
product of the war.

It was Nazi military success that first destroyed the prewar
status quo of Eastern Europe. Then it was the Nazis' military
failure that, to the applause of the Western Allies, drew Soviet military and political power into the resulting vacuum
and established it there, where it has remained ever since.
And it was the memory of the grievous injury done the Soviet
Union by the Germans while they were fighting in that country that caused the Soviet regime to consider it vital to its
security to retain ultimate control over at least the eastern
third of Germany and all intervening territory in order to
ensure that Russia would not again be confronted by a re-
armed and united Germany, possibly allied—this time—with
the United States.

This, in essence, was the origin of the Soviet Union's interest in Poland as we have known it over these past thirty-five
years. In the pursuit of this interest, Moscow has made many
and great mistakes. Some would deny the legitimacy of this
interest, but this is how the Soviet leaders perceive it, and it
is this interest that has been most prominent in their minds as
they stood by and witnessed, with growing alarm, the developments in Poland this past year.

To date, the Soviet Union has not intervened with its own

military forces. It was not the unending series of high-level warnings from Washington that motivated this restraint. The Kremlin obviously had weighty reasons of its own—it is not hard to imagine what they were—for not intervening.

One may assume that the only development that could drive the Russians to so drastic a step would be further degeneration of the Polish situation to a point where they saw their entire military and political hegemony in Eastern and Central Europe, including East Germany, being undermined, to the great detriment of their prestige and possibly of the internal stability of the Soviet Union itself. If they saw this happening, there is no telling what they would do.

If we really wanted to avert these and other dangers of an overanxious Soviet interest in the Polish political scene, then we must be willing to address ourselves to the Kremlin's basic strategic stake in the Eastern and Central European region. To do this, we would have to be prepared to re-examine the very terms on which the division of the continent has operated over the past three-and-a-half decades.

This would mean, at the outset, soundings and discussions to ascertain just what assurances Moscow would require, and what safeguards would have to be provided, to compensate for the loss of security that such a change of Soviet policy would signify in Soviet eyes.

We would then have to explore, together with our North Atlantic Treaty Organization allies, the possibilities for meeting these requirements. To be sure, it is unlikely that anything could bring Moscow to a point where it would disclaim any and all security interest in the state of affairs prevailing in Poland. But a certain relaxation of its demands, and, with it, a certain relaxation of existing tension, might be achieved if something could be done to give assurance that anything of this sort would not be taken advantage of by the NATO powers, to the detriment of the Soviet strategic position in Eastern and Central Europe as a whole.

The United States government cannot be unaware of this aspect of the problem, but to date its official pronouncements and actions seem to have taken no account of it. Is it not high time that this omission be corrected? Otherwise, we run the danger—and it is a serious one—of driving the Soviet leadership to desperation by pressing it mercilessly against a closed door. (*New York Times* Op-Ed article, 1/6/82.)

3

THE
NUCLEAR
AGE IN
CRISIS

12

A PROPOSAL FOR INTERNATIONAL DISARMAMENT

(1981)

Adequate words are lacking to express the full seriousness of our present situation. It is not just that we are for the moment on a collision course politically with the Soviet Union, and that the process of rational communication between the two governments seems to have broken down completely; it is also—and even more importantly—the fact that the ultimate sanction behind the conflicting policies of these two governments is a type and volume of weaponry which could not possibly be used without utter disaster for us all.

For over thirty years, wise and far-seeing people have been warning us about the futility of any war fought with nuclear weapons and about the dangers involved in their cultivation. Some of the first of these voices to be raised were those of great scientists, including outstandingly that of Albert Einstein himself. But there has been no lack of others. Every president of this country, from Dwight Eisenhower to Jimmy Carter, has tried to remind us that there could be no such thing as victory in a war fought with such weapons. So have a great many other eminent persons.

When one looks back today over the history of these warnings, one has the impression that something has now been lost of the sense of urgency, the hopes, and the excitement that initially inspired them, so many years ago. One senses, even on the part of those who today most acutely perceive the problem and are inwardly most exercised about it, a certain discouragement, resignation, perhaps even despair, when it comes to the question of raising the subject again. The danger is so obvious. So much has already been said. What is to be gained by reiteration? What good would it now do?

Look at the record. Over all these years the competition in the development of nuclear weaponry has proceeded steadily, relentlessly, without the faintest regard for all these warning voices. We have gone on piling weapon upon weapon, missile upon missile, new levels of destructiveness upon old ones. We have done this helplessly, almost involuntarily: like the victims of some sort of hypnotism, like men in a dream, like lemmings heading for the sea, like the children of Hamlin marching blindly along behind their Pied Piper. And the result is that today we have achieved, we and the Russians together, in the creation of these devices and their means of delivery, levels of redundancy of such grotesque dimensions as to defy rational understanding.

I say redundancy. I know of no better way to describe it. But actually, the word is too mild. It implies that there could be levels of these weapons that would not be redundant. Personally, I doubt that there could. I question whether these devices are really weapons at all. A true weapon is at best something with which you endeavor to affect the behavior of another society by influencing the minds, the calculations, the intentions, of the men that control it; it is not something with which you destroy indiscriminately the lives, the substance, the hopes, the culture, the civilization, of another people.

What a confession of intellectual poverty it would be—what a bankruptcy of intelligent statesmanship—if we had to admit that such blind, senseless acts of destruction were the best use we could make of what we have come to view as the leading elements of our military strength!

To my mind, the nuclear bomb is the most useless weapon ever invented. It can be employed to no rational purpose. It is not even an effective defense against itself. It is only something with which, in a moment of petulance or panic, you commit such fearful acts of destruction as no sane person would ever wish to have upon his conscience.

There are those who will agree, with a sigh, to much of what I have just said, but will point to the need for something called deterrence. This is, of course, a concept which attributes to others—to others who, like ourselves, were born of women, walk on two legs, and love their children, to human beings, in short—the most fiendish and inhuman of tendencies.

But all right: accepting for the sake of argument the profound iniquity of these adversaries, no one could deny, I think, that the present Soviet and American arsenals, presenting over a million times the destructive power of the Hiroshima bomb, are simply fantastically redundant to the purpose in question. If the same relative proportions were to be preserved, something well less than 20 percent of those stocks would surely suffice for the most sanguine concepts of deterrence, whether as between the two nuclear superpowers or with relation to any of those other governments that have been so ill-advised as to enter upon the nuclear path. Whatever their suspicions of each other, there can be no excuse on the part of these two governments for holding, poised against each other and poised in a sense against the whole Northern Hemisphere, quantities of these weapons so vastly in excess of any rational and demonstrable requirements.

How have we got ourselves into this dangerous mess?

Let us not confuse the question by blaming it all on our Soviet adversaries. They have, of course, their share of the blame, and not least in their cavalier dismissal of the Baruch Plan so many years ago. They too have made their mistakes; and I should be the last to deny it.

But we must remember that it has been we Americans who, at almost every step of the road, have taken the lead in the development of this sort of weaponry. It was we who first produced and tested such a device; we who were the first to raise its destructiveness to a new level with the hydrogen bomb; we who introduced the multiple warhead; we who have declined every proposal for the renunciation of the principle of "first use"; and we alone, so help us God, who have used the weapon in anger against others, and against tens of thousands of helpless noncombatants at that.

I know that reasons were offered for some of these things. I know that others might have taken this sort of a lead, had we not done so. But let us not, in the face of this record, so lose ourselves in self-righteousness and hypocrisy as to forget our own measure of complicity in creating the situation we face today.

What is it then, if not our own will, and if not the supposed wickedness of our opponents, that has brought us to this pass?

The answer, I think, is clear. It is primarily the inner momentum, the independent momentum, of the weapons race itself—the compulsions that arise and take charge of great powers when they enter upon a competition with each other in the building up of major armaments of any sort.

This is nothing new. I am a diplomatic historian. I see this same phenomenon playing its fateful part in the relations among the great European powers as much as a century ago. I see this competitive buildup of armaments conceived initially as a means to an end but soon becoming the end itself. I see it taking possession of men's imagination and behavior, becoming a force in its own right, detaching itself from the political differences that initially inspired it, and then leading both parties, invariably and inexorably, to the war they no longer know how to avoid.

This is a species of fixation, brewed out of many components. There are fears, resentments, national pride, personal pride. There are misreadings of the adversary's intentions— sometimes even the refusal to consider them at all. There is the tendency of national communities to idealize themselves and to dehumanize the opponent. There is the blinkered, narrow vision of the professional military planner, and his tendency to make war inevitable by assuming its inevitability.

Tossed together, these components form a powerful brew. They guide the fears and the ambitions of men. They seize the policies of governments and whip them around like trees before the tempest.

Is it possible to break out of this charmed and vicious circle? It is sobering to recognize that no one, at least to my knowledge, has yet done so. But no one, for that matter, has ever been faced with such great catastrophe, such inalterable catastrophe, at the end of the line. Others, in earlier decades, could befuddle themselves with dreams of something called "victory." We, perhaps fortunately, are denied this seductive prospect. We have to break out of the circle. We have no other choice.

How are we to do it?

I must confess that I see no possibility of doing this by means of discussions along the lines of the negotiations that have been in progress, off and on, over this past decade, under the acronym of SALT. I regret, to be sure, that the most recent SALT agreement has not been ratified. I regret it, because if the benefits to be expected from that agreement were slight, its disadvantages were even slighter; and it had a symbolic value which should not have been so lightly sacrificed.

But I have, I repeat, no illusion that negotiations on the SALT pattern—negotiations, that is, in which each side is obsessed with the chimera of relative advantage and strives only to retain a maximum of the weaponry for itself while putting its opponent to the maximum disadvantage—I have no illusion that such negotiations could ever be adequate to get us out of this hole. They are not a way of escape from the weapons race; they are an integral part of it.

Whoever does not understand that when it comes to nuclear weapons the whole concept of relative advantage is illusory— whoever does not understand that when you are talking about absurd and preposterous quantities of overkill the relative sizes of arsenals have no serious meaning—whoever does not understand that the danger lies, not in the possibility that someone else might have more missiles and warheads than we do, but in the very existence of these unconscionable quantities of highly poisonous explosives, and their existence, above all, in hands as weak and shaky and undependable as those of ourselves or our adversaries or any other mere human beings: whoever does not understand these things is never going to guide us out of this increasingly dark and meancing forest of bewilderments into which we have all wandered.

I can see no way out of this dilemma other than by a bold

and sweeping departure, a departure that would cut surgically through the exaggerated anxieties, the self-engendered nightmares, and the sophisticated mathematics of destruction in which we have all been entangled over these recent years, and would permit us to move, with courage and decision, to the heart of the problem.

President Reagan recently said, and I think very wisely, that he would "negotiate as long as necessary to reduce the numbers of nuclear weapons to a point where neither side threatens the survival of the other."

Now that is, of course, precisely the thought to which these present observations of mine are addressed. But I wonder whether the negotiations would really have to be at such great length. What I would like to see the president do, after due consultation with the Congress, would be to propose to the Soviet government an immediate across-the-boards reduction by 50 percent of the nuclear arsenals now being maintained by the two superpowers; a reduction affecting in equal measure all forms of the weapon, strategic, medium-range, and tactical, as well as all means of their delivery: all this to be implemented at once and without further wrangling among the experts, and to be subject to such national means of verification as now lie at the disposal of the two powers.

Whether the balance of reduction would be precisely even —whether it could be construed to favor statistically one side or the other—would not be the question. Once we start thinking that way, we would be back on the same old fateful track that has brought us where we are today. Whatever the precise results of such a reduction, there would still be plenty of overkill left—so much so that if this first operation were successful, I would then like to see a second one put in hand to rid us of at least two-thirds of what would be left.

Now I have, of course, no idea of the scientific aspects of such an operation; but I can imagine that serious problems might be presented by the task of removing, and disposing safely of, the radioactive contents of the many thousands of warheads that would have to be dismantled. Should this be the case, I would like to see the president couple his appeal for a

50 percent reduction with the proposal that there be established a joint Soviet-American scientific committee, under the chairmanship of a distinguished netural figure, to study jointly and in all humility the problem not only of the safe disposal of these wastes but also of how they could be utilized in such a way as to make a positive contribution to human life, either in the two countries themselves or—perhaps preferably—elsewhere. In such a joint scientific venture we might both atone for some of our past follies and lay the foundation for a more constructive relationship.

It will be said this proposal, whatever its merits, deals with only a part of the problem. This is perfectly true. Behind it there would still lurk the serious political differences that now divide us from the Soviet government. Behind it would still lie the problems recently treated, and still to be treated, in the SALT forum. Behind it would still lie the great question of the acceptability of war itself, any war, even a conventional one, as a means of solving problems among great industrial powers in this age of high technology.

What has been suggested here would not prejudice the continued treatment of these questions just as they might be treated today, in whatever forums and under whatever safeguards the two powers find necessary. The conflicts and arguments over these questions could all still proceed to the heart's content of all those who view them with such passionate commitment. The stakes would simply be smaller; and that would be a great relief to all of us.

What I have suggested is, of course, only a beginning. But a beginning has to be made somewhere; and if it has to be made, is it not best that it should be made where the dangers are the greatest, and their necessity the least? If a step of this nature could be successfully taken, people might find the heart to tackle with greater confidence and determination the many problems that would still remain.

It will also be argued that there would be risks involved. Possibly so. I do not see them. I do not deny the possibility. But if there are, so what? Is it possible to conceive of any dangers greater than those that lie at the end of the collision course on which we are now embarked? And if not, why choose the greater—why choose, in fact, the greatest—of all risks, in the hopes of avoiding the lesser ones?

We are confronted here, my friends, with two courses. At the end of the one lies hope—faint hope, if you will, uncertain hope, hope surrounded with dangers, if you insist. At the end of the other lies, so far as I am able to see, no hope at all.

Can there be—in the light of our duty not just to ourselves (for we are all going to die sooner or later) but of our duty to our own kind, our duty to the continuity of the generations, our duty to the great experiment of civilized life on this rare and rich and marvelous planet—can there be, in the light of these claims on our loyalty, any question as to which course we should adopt?

In the final week of his life, Albert Einstein signed the last of the collective appeals against the development of nuclear weapons that he was ever to sign. He was dead before it appeared. It was an appeal drafted, I gather, by Bertrand Russell. I had my differences with Russell at the time as I do now in retrospect; but I would like to quote one sentence from the final paragraph of that statement, not only because it was the last one Einstein ever signed, but because it sums up, I think, all that I have to say on the subject. It reads as follows:

> We appeal, as human beings to human beings: Remember your humanity, and forget the rest.

(Speech delivered on receipt of the Albert Einstein Peace Prize, 5/19/81.)

13

THE
ALTERNATIVES
WE FACE

(1981)

I think you all know that I am not in any sense an expert on the subject of arms development or arms control. I am not connected with any strategic think-tank. My working hours are devoted to diplomatic history—and diplomatic history, at that, of a period when people were mercifully innocent of any involvement with nuclear weaponry. I am only a private citizen, who reads a certain amount of what appears on these subjects in the public prints, and occasionally, in his spare moments, even makes notes on what he reads. I can, therefore, only give you a brief summary of some of my personal impressions.

Since I am a historian, you must first let me go back a bit in time, and observe that the strategy of waging war against entire populations as well as against just the armed forces of a military adversary is of very recent adoption. It first came into currency in World War I. In World War II it was embraced by both sides with enthusiasm. It included, as a major feature, the bombing of urban areas and industrial centers. Our use of the atomic weapon against Japan in 1945 was therefore only an extrapolation of what we had been doing with conventional ones; and I suppose it came naturally to people to make this extrapolation, particularly to military people, who tend to believe that relative distinctions are not important and that the more destructive a weapon is, the more effective—even when the destructiveness becomes suicidal.

Be that as it may, having taken the lead in the development and use of nuclear weapons, having persistently ignored their obviously suicidal implications, feeling initially that we had an unshakable superiority in them, and seeing in them an easy alternative to the politically uncomfortable burden of maintaining adequate conventional forces in peacetime, we embraced nuclear weapons with enthusiasm, used them against the Japanese, took them to our hearts, and unwisely based our military posture very extensively upon their cultivation. And having done this, we proceeded to destroy not only our moral position but our possibilities for effective leadership in efforts for nuclear arms control by declining to renounce the principle of "first use"—by insistently reserving to ourselves, that is, the option of using these weapons in any serious military encounter, regardless of whether they were or were not used against us.

This last fact had, I believe, a fundamental causal relationship to our present troubles and dangers. A government which bases its own plans and preparations on the first use of nuclear weapons can never expect to exert any useful leadership in the effort to bring this form of weaponry under international control.

I tried, without success, to make all this clear to my superiors in government some thirty-one years ago. The issue at that time was whether we should build the hydrogen bomb. I tried to persuade those superiors that in going ahead with the cultivation of nuclear weaponry and at the same time reserving to ourselves the option of being the first to use it even when it was not used against us, we were sowing the seeds of much future trouble and inviting the emergence of dilemmas, in the face of which public opinion someday would be unable to understand or support our statesmanship. I see no reason, today, to regret those warnings. That unhappy day, I suspect, is now approaching. I continue to believe that the invidious insistence on the option of first use of the weapon lies at the heart of our helplessness and ineffectiveness before the dangers of a growing weapons race, and that we will not be able to develop a hopeful and effective policy either in the field of arms control or on the question of nuclear proliferation until we take a deep breath and consent to believe that we could exist, and should be prepared to exist, in a world where nuclear weapons were not part of the picture.

In this connection let me point out a certain aspect of irony in our official position on these matters. We declare, and endlessly assert, that our nuclear forces are maintained for the sole necessity of deterring the Soviet government from launching nuclear strikes against us or our allies. Now the Soviet government, unlike ourselves, did not take the lead in developing this kind of weaponry. It has never used nuclear weapons in anger against anyone. It has repeatedly called for an international agreement committing all the parties to a firm renunciation of the principle of "first use," thus affirming its own readiness to accept this principle if we would do likewise. Only a fortnight ago, Mr. Gromyko proposed in the United Nations an Assembly resolution declaring such first use of nuclear weapons to be an international crime. We, on the other hand, who *have* used the weapon in anger, and who are even today unwilling to renounce the option of its first use, then say that we must have more and more nuclear weapons in order to deter the Soviet Union from launching a nuclear attack on us. Is there not a certain contradiction here? If our only purpose in deploying the weapons is to "deter" others from using them, which would seem to imply that we had no intention of being the first to do so—that we would use them only for retaliation—why then cling to the option of "first use"? Could not the others say, with even greater logic, that we are the ones who have to be deterred?

However, going on from there: it is my impression, and one which I believe I share with a great many thoughtful people, that after thirty-five years of trying to base our security on this kind of weaponry, and this sort of policy with relation to it, we have succeeded only in creating, and in stimulating our adversaries to join us in creating, an utterly grotesque amount of nuclear overkill—vast quantities of nuclear arms which could not conceivably be used for any purposes other than one so insanely disastrous that no man in his right mind would wish to have the responsibility for pursuing it—a volume of overkill so preposterous, in fact, that the mere existence of it, given the possibilities for error, accident, sabotage, and escape into other hands, represents a danger to the entire civilization of the Northern Hemisphere. And in the face of this situation, our government has found nothing better to do than to reject the only negotiated agreement that might have placed at least moderate limits to the further momentum of the weapons race —namely, the second SALT agreement—and to indulge itself in the assumption that by further multiplying this overkill, we can somehow or other make ourselves more secure.

I think I know the reasoning behind this policy. I know that some of our drawing-board strategists profess to see a so-called window of vulnerability through which, at some date several years in the future, the Soviets could, if they wanted to, "take out," as the euphemistic phrase goes, our land-based missiles by a single surgical strike, thus leaving us in a helpless position where we would not dare to retaliate with those missiles that had not been taken out and would therefore have to accept Soviet dictation—or, as the more dramatic phrase has it, to "surrender."

Time does not permit me to analyze critically this curious process of reasoning. I shall only say that it is predicated on such wild and implausible scenarios, involves so fantastic a view of the monstrosity of our Soviet adversaries, omits so many obviously relevant considerations, and reflects so childish a conception of the way great governments are motivated and behave that I find myself thinking there must be something of great importance that I have missed; otherwise the conclusions I would have to draw about the state of mind of our strategists in Washington are ones I would not like to describe on this occasion.

It may be asked: Are there no conceivable alternatives to the course upon which we are now embarked—no alternatives, that is, which ought at least to be receiving serious considera-tion both in governmental circles and in our public discussions? The answer is: Of course there are. We could accept the commitment not to be the first to use these weapons in combat. We could press for a comprehensive test ban, an objective towards which we have already advanced partway and which, if achieved, could perhaps do more than anything else to bring about at least a stabilization of the nuclear balance. We could explore seriously the possibility for deep cuts in the strategic arsenals. We could similarly explore the possibilities for a total denuclearization of Central and Northern Europe.

But these alternatives seem to be either ignored or given a very low priority at the executive level of government. Congress seems to be either reluctant or too busy to occupy itself with them. They are given very little attention in the press and the public media. Our press seems, in fact, to have lost its faculty for vigorous critical response when it comes to these questions. And public opinion, particularly informed opinion, seems to have been overcome by a sense of hopeless fatalism, by a feeling that there is nothing that can be done, that we can only wait passively, let our government go ahead with its plans for increasing the scale and pace of the weapons race, and hope against hope for the best.

The result, as you all know, is that not only is this weapons race now proceeding at a dizzy pace, but there is real danger that it will soon grow totally out of control. This is because the principle of mutual vulnerability on which the earlier SALT accords were based is now being rapidly eroded by the introduction of new technologies which complicate the problem of verification and which raise the dangers, and above all the apparent perceived dangers, of the development of "first strike" capabilities on both sides.

I cannot tell you how seriously I view this state of affairs. It is not just that Soviet-American relations are at the lowest point in thirty years—at a point where there is very little cushion of mutual understanding and communication to absorb any unexpected shocks. It is not just that the present weapons race plus political tension bears all the earmarks of the situations which have relentlessly led to great wars in the past. It is also the fact that we have, in several parts of the world where the interests of the two superpowers are now heavily engaged, situations of extreme instability where complications could spring up at any moment, complications which neither of the superpowers may have provoked or desired or even foreseen; and where these complications might nevertheless create highly fragile and tense crises, in the face of which neither superpower would feel itself in a position to avoid the resort to armed measures. I don't want to be an alarmist; but it seems to me that the most casual scrutiny of our world situation will suggest that we are sitting on a tinder box—and one where the nature of the tinder is infinitely more menacing than anything the world has heretofore known. I would be happy if developments would prove me to be overly pessimistic. But that is the situation, as I see it.

DENUCLEAR-
IZATION

(1981)

The Reagan administration is now committed to entering into talks with the Soviet Union, at the end of next month, on the question of the so-called theater nuclear weapons in and around Central Europe. Let us hope that in preparing its negotiating position, the administration will consider that alternative which, precisely because it is the simplest, may also appear the most radical: namely, total denuclearization of the region.

There would seem to be two kinds of settlements at which the United States delegation could conceivably aim. One would be predicated on the deployment of *some* American theater nuclear weapons on Western European territory, and would merely seek agreement with the Soviet side on the numbers, characteristics, and areas of deployment of these weapons and of the similar Soviet ones trained on Western Europe. This alternative would represent an effort to agree with Moscow only on the limitation, not the elimination, of the theater nuclear weapons to be deployed in the region.

The second alternative would be to seek the total denuclearization of Central and Northern Europe, in the sense that it would require the elimination of all land-based nuclear weapons stationed or trained on that region. This would of course mean the verifiable removal by the Soviet side of its so-called SS-20s and the older missiles they are replacing. It would mean the similar removal of the six-thousand-odd so-called tactical nuclear weapons that the United States is understood to have deployed in West Germany—presumably no great sacrifice on our part, if what we hear about the obsolescence and general uselessness of these weapons is correct. It would preclude the deployment of any further nuclear weapons in or around the region.

This solution would have important advantages for all concerned.

First, it would be a clean solution, relatively easily verifiable. It is easier, after all, to verify an absence of all nuclear weapons than an absence of some.

For Moscow, it would have the advantages both of eliminating the United States tactical weapons now deployed in West Germany and of obviating any further deployments of American nuclear weapons there.

For the Europeans, this solution would remove the nightmare of the Soviet medium-range missiles now trained on Central and Northern Europe. It would meet the feelings of the majority of Scandinavians, who have never had nuclear weapons stationed on their soil and are determined to avoid this in the future, and would obviate the demand for a special Nordic nuclear-free zone. Several of the European NATO governments, outstandingly that of West Germany, would find themselves relieved of the powerful and growing pressures from elements in their own populations that have strong objections to the stationing of any sort of nuclear weapons on their territories, and with this relief would also disappear the serious threat to NATO's unity that those pressures pose.

There would, to everyone's relief, be no further question of deploying the neutron bomb in West Germany or anywhere else in the region.

Finally, and of no small importance at this particular moment, a good deal of money would be saved, all around.

What are the objections?

It may be argued that the Soviet side would not accept it. To which may be replied: Until one tries it, one will never know. Leonid I. Brezhnev has repeatedly indicated readiness to make serious concessions in return just for a delay in the proposed American deployments. The prospect of the removal of the American tactical warheads—to my knowledge, this has never been offered from our side—should be an added incentive, and an American agreement not to deploy further nuclear weapons in that region would be an even greater one. There would no doubt be complications to be faced and questions to be resolved with regard to this or any other proposal we might make to Moscow in this connection, but it is most unlikely that the Soviet side would reject out of hand a proposal that meets in so high a degree its principal concerns.

It may also be argued that the absence of American nuclear weapons in West Germany would leave the entire region helpless in the face of Soviet superiority in conventional arms. There are some of us who would challenge the assumptions about Soviet capabilities and intentions on which that objection rests. But in any case, a determined strengthening of the North Atlantic Treaty Organization's conventional capabilities in that area (and not just in fancy new equipment but in discipline, morale, training, numbers, and general quality of personnel) is already overdue; and it would, for many reasons, be a better answer to the problem of Soviet superiority than a program of further nuclear deployments that threaten to raise the nuclear-weapons race to new levels of redundancy and danger, and to tear NATO to pieces in the process.

This approach would neither preclude nor would it render unnecessary the effort to bring about deep cuts in the long-range strategic Soviet and American arsenals.

On the contrary, it would be a necessary complement to that effort. Nor would the need for something along these lines be affected by further complications of the Polish problem.

The issues at stake are ones that would continue to exist and would demand treatment regardless of the momentary state of relations between the Soviet Union and the United States.

The effort to control and abate the nuclear weapons race is not, after all, a favor we are doing for the Russians any more than it is a favor to ourselves. It is a dictate of the security and survival of all Western civilization. Let us first meet that dictate. The rest can come afterward. (*New York Times* Op-Ed article, 10/11/81.)

ON
NUCLEAR
WAR

(1981)

The recent growth and gathering strength of the anti-nuclear-war movement here and in Europe is to my mind the most striking phenomenon of this beginning of the 1980s. It is all the more impressive because it is so extensively spontaneous. It has already achieved dimensions which will make it impossible, I think, for the respective governments to ignore it. It will continue to grow until something is done to meet it.

Like any great spontaneous popular movement, this one has, and must continue to have, its ragged edges, and even its dangers. It will attract the freaks and the extremists. Many of the wrong people will attach themselves to it. It will wander off in mistaken directions and become confused with other causes that are less worthy. It already shows need of leadership and of centralized organization.

But it is idle to try to stamp it, as some have done, as a Communist-inspired movement. Of course, Communists try to get into the act. Of course, they exploit the movement wherever they can. These are routine political tactics. But actually, I see no signs that the Communist input into this great public reaction has been of any decisive significance.

Nor is it useful to portray the entire European wing of this movement as the expression of some sort of vague and naïvely neutralist sentiment. There is some of that, certainly; but where there is, it is largely a reaction to the negative and hopeless quality of our own Cold War policies, which seem to envisage nothing other than an indefinitely increasing political tension and nuclear danger. It is not surprising that many Europeans should see no salvation for themselves in so sterile a perspective and should cast about for something that would have in it some positive element—some ray of hope.

Least of all does this neutralist sentiment necessarily represent any timorous desire to accept Soviet authority as a way of avoiding the normal responsibilities of national defense. The cliché of "better Red than dead" is a facile and clever phrase; but actually, no one in Europe is faced with such a choice, or is likely to be. We will not be aided in our effort to understand Europe's problems by distortions of this nature. Our government will have to recognize that there are a great many people who would accept the need for adequate national defense but who would emphatically deny that the nuclear weapon, and particularly the first use of that weapon, is anything with which a country should or could defend itself.

No: this movement against nuclear armaments and nuclear war may be ragged and confused and disorganized, but at the heart of it lie some very fundamental and reasonable and powerful motivations: among them a growing appreciation by many people of the true horrors of a nuclear war; a determination not to see their children deprived of life, or their civilization destroyed, by a holocaust of this nature; and finally, as Grenville Clark said, a very real exasperation with their governments for the rigidity and traditionalism that cause those governments to ignore the fundamental distinction between conventional weapons and the weapons of mass destruction and prevent them from finding, or even seriously seeking, ways of escape from the fearful trap into which the cultivation of nuclear weapons is leading us.

Such considerations are not the reflections of Communist propaganda. They are not the products of some sort of timorous neutralism. They are the expression of a deep instinctive insistence, if you don't mind, on sheer survival—on survival as individuals, as parents, as members of a civilization.

Our government will ignore this fact at its peril. This move-

ment is too powerful, too elementary, too deeply embedded in
the natural human instinct for self-preservation, to be brushed
aside. Sooner or later, and the sooner the better, all the governments on both sides of the East-West division will find
themselves compelled to undertake the search for positive
alternatives to the insoluble dilemmas which any suicidal form
of weaponry presents, and can only present.

Do such alternatives exist?

Of course they do. One does not have to go far to look for
them. A start could be made with deep cuts in the long-range
strategic missilery. There could be a complete denuclearization
of Central and Northern Europe. There could be a complete
ban on nuclear testing. At the very least, one could accept a
temporary freeze on the further buildup of these fantasstic
arsenals. None of this would undermine anyone's security.

These alternatives, obviously, are not ones that we in the
West could expect to realize all by ourselves. I am not suggesting any unilateral disarmament. Plainly, two—and eventually
even more than two—will have to play at this game.

And even these alternatives would be only a beginning. But
they would be a tremendously hopeful beginning. And what I
am suggesting is that one should at least begin to explore them
—and to explore them with a good will and a courage and an
imagination the signs of which I fail, as yet, to detect on the
part of those in Washington who have our destinies in their
hands.

This, then, in my opinion, is what ought to be done—what
will, someday, have to be done. But for this country the change
will not come easily, even in the best of circumstances. It is not
something that could be accomplished from one day to the
next by any simple one-time decision. What is involved in the
effort to turn these things around is a fundamental and extensive change in our prevailing outlooks on a number of points,
and an extensive restructuring of our entire defense posture.

We would have to begin by accepting the validity of two
very fundamental appreciations. The first is that there is no
issue at stake in our political relations with the Soviet Union

—no hope, no fear, nothing to which we aspire, nothing we would like to avoid—which could conceivably be worth a nuclear war. And the second is that there is no way in which nuclear weapons could conceivably be employed in combat that would not involve the possibility—and indeed the prohibitively high probability—of escalation into a general nuclear disaster.

If we can once get these two truths into our heads, then the next thing we will have to do is to abandon the option to which we have stubbornly clung for thirty years: the first use of nuclear weapons in any military encounter. This flows with iron logic from the two propositions I have just enunciated. First use of these weapons has long been rendered irrational by the ability of the USSR to respond in kind. The insistence on this option of first use has corrupted and vitiated our entire policy on nuclear matters ever since these weapons were first developed. I am persuaded that we shall never be able to exert a constructive leadership in matters of nuclear arms reduction or in the problem of nuclear proliferation until this pernicious and indefensible position is abandoned.

And once it *has* been abandoned, there will presumably have to be a far-reaching restructuring of our armed forces. The private citizen is of course not fully informed in such matters; and I don't pretend to be. But from all that has become publicly known, one can only suppose that nearly all aspects of the training and equipment of those armed forces, not to mention the strategy and tactics underlying their operations, have been affected by the assumption that we might have to fight—indeed, might wish to fight—with nuclear weapons, and that we might well be the ones to inaugurate their use.

A great deal of this would presumably have to be turned around—not all of it, but much of it, nevertheless. We might, so long as others retained such weapons, have to retain them ourselves for purposes of deterrence and reassurance to our people, and other peoples. But we could no longer rely on them for any positive purpose even in the case of reverses on the conventional battlefield; and our forces would have to be trained and equipped accordingly: that is, to defend us successfully with conventional weapons. Personally, this would cause me no pain. But let no one suppose that the change would come easily. An enormous inertia exists here and would have to be overcome; and in my experience there is no inertia, once established, as formidable as that of the armed services. Far-reaching changes may also be required in such things as discipline, training, and above all method of recruitment of the ground forces.

But there is something else, too, that will have to be altered, in my opinion, if we are to move things around and take a more constructive posture; and that is the view of the Soviet Union and its peoples to which our governmental establishment and a large part of our journalistic establishment have seemed recently to be committed.

On this point, I would particularly like not to be misunderstood. I do not have, and have never had, any sympathy for the ideology of the Soviet leadership. I know that this is a regime with which it is not possible for us to have a fully satisfactory relationship. I know that there are many important matters on which no collaboration between us is possible, just as there are other matters on which we can collaborate. There are a number of Soviet habits and practices that I deeply deplore, and that I feel we should resist firmly when they impinge on our interests. I recognize, too, that the Soviet leadership does not always act in its own best interests—that it is capable of making mistakes, and that Afghanistan is one of those mistakes, and one which it will come to regret, regardless of anything we may do to punish it.

Finally, I recognize that there has recently been a drastic and very serious deterioration of Soviet-American relations, and that this may well be exacerbated by any worsening of the Polish situation. This deterioration is a fact in itself and something which it will not be easy to correct; for it has led to new commitments and attitudes of embitterment and suspicion on both sides. The almost exclusive militarization of thinking and discourse about Soviet-American relations that now commands the Washington atmosphere and a good deal of our press—a militarization which, it sometimes seems to me, could not be different if we knew for a fact that we were unquestionably to be at war with the Soviet Union within a matter of months: this in itself is a dangerous state of affairs, which it is not going to be easy to correct. So I don't think I underestimate the gravity of the problem.

But, all this being said, I must go on and say that I find the view of the Soviet Union that prevails today in large portions of our governmental and journalistic establishments so extreme, so subjective, so far removed from what any sober scrutiny of external reality would reveal, that it is not only ineffective but dangerous as a guide to political action.

This endless series of distortions and oversimplifications; this systematic dehumanization of the leadership of another great country; this routine exaggeration of Moscow's military capabilities and of the supposed iniquity of Soviet intentions; this monotonous misrepresentation of the nature and the attitudes of another great people—and a long-suffering people at that, sorely tried by the vicissitudes of this past century; this ignoring of their pride, their hopes—yes, even of their illusions (for they have their illusions, just as we have ours; and illusions, too, deserve respect); this reckless application of the double standard to the judgment of Soviet conduct and our own; this failure to recognize, finally, the communality of many of their problems and ours as we both move inexorably into the modern technological age; and this corresponding tendency to view all aspects of the relationship in terms of a supposed total and irreconcilable conflict of concerns and of aims: these, believe me, are not the marks of the maturity and discrimination one expects of the diplomacy of a great power; they are the marks of an intellectual primitivism and naïvety unpardonable in a great government. I use the word naïvety, because there is a naivety of cynicism and suspicion just as there is a naïvety of innocence.

And we shall not be able to turn these things around as they should be turned, on the plane of military and nuclear rivalry, until we learn to correct these childish distortions—until we correct our tendency to see in the Soviet Union only a mirror in which we look for the reflection of our own virtue—until we consent to see there another great people, one of the world's greatest, in all its complexity and variety, embracing the good with the bad, a people whose life, whose views, whose habits, whose fears and aspirations, whose successes and failures, are the products, just as ours are the products, not of any inherent iniquity but of the relentless discipline of history, tradition, and national experience. Above all, we must learn to see the behavior of the leadership of that country as partly the reflection of our own treatment of it. If we insist on demonizing these Soviet leaders—on viewing them as total and incorrigible enemies, consumed only with their fear or hatred of us and dedicated to nothing other than our destruction—that, in the end, is the way we shall assuredly have them, if for no other reason than that our view of them allows for nothing else, either for them or for us.

These, then, are the changes we shall have to make—the changes in our concept of the relationship of nuclear weaponry to national defense, changes in the structure and training and spirit of our armed forces, changes in our view of the distant country which our military planners seem to have selected as our inevitable and inalterable enemy—if we hope to reverse the dreadful trend towards a final nuclear conflagration. And it is urgently important that we get on with these changes. Time is not waiting for us. The fragile nuclear balance that has prevailed in recent years is rapidly being undermined, not so much by the steady buildup of the nuclear arsenals on both sides (for they already represent nothing more than preposterous accumulations of overkill), but rather by technological advances that threaten to break down the verifiability of the respective capabilities and to stimulate the fears, the temptations, and the compulsions of a "first strike" mentality. We are getting very close to that today.

But it is important for another reason, too, that we get on with these changes. For beyond all this, beyond the shadow of the atom and its horrors, there lie other problems—tremendous problems—that demand our attention almost as urgently.

There are the great environmental complications now beginning to close in on us: the question of what we are doing to the world oceans with our pollution, the problem of the greenhouse effect, the acid rains, the question of what is happening to the topsoil and the ecology and the water supplies of this and other countries. And there are the profound spiritual problems that spring from the complexity and artificiality of the modern urban-industrial society, problems that confront the Russians and ourselves alike, and to which neither of us has as yet responded very well. One sees on every hand the signs of our common failure. One sees it in the cynicism and apathy and drunkenness of so much of the Soviet population. One sees it in the crime and drug abuse and general decay and degradation of our city centers. To some extent—not entirely but extensively—these failures have their origins in experiences common to both of us.

And these problems, too, will not wait. Unless we both do better in dealing with them than we have done to date, even the banishment of the nuclear danger will not help us very much.

Can we not at long last cast off our preoccupation with sheer destruction, a preoccupation that is costing us our prosperity and pre-empting the resources that should go to the solving of our great social problems, to the progress of our respective societies? Is it really impossible for us to cast off this sickness of blind military rivalry and to address ourselves at last, in all humility and in all seriousness, to setting our societies to rights?

For this entire preoccupation with nuclear war is a form of illness. It is morbid in the extreme. There is no hope in it—only horror. It can be understood only as some form of subconscious despair on the part of its devotees—some sort of death wish, a readiness to commit suicide for fear of death—a state of mind explicable only by some inability to face the normal hazards and vicissitudes of the human predicament—a lack of faith, or better a lack of the very strength that it takes to have faith, as countless of our generations have had it before us.

I decline to believe that this is the condition of the majority of our people. Surely there is among us, at least among the majority of us, a sufficient health of the spirit, a sufficient affirmation of life, with all its joys and excitements and all its hazards and uncertainties, to permit us to slough off this morbid preoccupation, to see it and discard it as the illness it is, to turn our attention to the real challenges and possibilities that loom beyond it, and in this way to restore to ourselves our confidence in ourselves and our hope for the future of the civilization to which we all belong. (Speech delivered on receipt of the Grenville Clark Prize, 11/16/81, at Dartmouth College.)

A CHRISTIAN'S
VIEW
OF THE
ARMS RACE

(1982)

The public discussion of the problems presented by nuclear weaponry which is now taking place in this country is going to go down in history, I suspect (assuming, of course, that history is to continue at all and does not itself fall victim to the sort of weaponry we are discussing), as the most significant that any democratic society has ever engaged in.

I myself have participated from time to time in this discussion, whenever I thought I might usefully do so; but in doing so, I have normally been speaking only in my capacity as a citizen talking to other citizens; and since not all of those other citizens were Christians, I did not feel that I could appeal directly to Christian values. Instead, I have tried only to invoke those values which, as it seemed to me, had attained the quality of accepted ideals of our society as a whole.

In this article, I would like to address myself to some of these same problems more strictly from the Christian standpoint. I do this with some hesitation, because while I hold myself to be a Christian, in the imperfect way that so many others do, I am certainly no better a one than millions of others; and I can claim no erudition whatsoever in the field of Christian theology. If, therefore, I undertake to look at the problems of nuclear weaponry from a Christian standpoint, I am aware that the standpoint, in this instance, is a primitive one, theologically speaking, and that this places limitations on its value. This is, however, the way that a great many of us have to look at the subject; and if primitive paintings are conceded to have some aesthetic value, perhaps the same sort of indulgence can be granted to a layperson's view of the relationship of nuclear weaponry to his own faith.

I

There are, I believe, two ways in which one may view the nuclear weapon, so-called. One way is to view it just as one more weapon, like any other weapon, only more destructive. This is the way it is generally viewed, I am afraid, by our miitary authorities and by many others. I personally do not see it this way. A weapon is something that is supposed to serve some rational end—a hideous end, as a rule, but one related to some serious objective of governmental policy, one supposed to promote the interests of the society which employs it. The nuclear device seems to me not to respond to that description.

But for those who do see it this way I would like to point out that if it is to be considered a weapon like other weapons, then it must be subjected to the same restraints, to the same rules of warfare, which were supposed, by international law and treaty, to apply to other forms of weaponry. One of these was the prescription that weapons should be employed in a manner calculated to bring an absolute minimum of hardship to non-combatants and to the entire infrastructure of civilian life. This principle was of course offended against in the most serious way in World War II; and our nuclear strategists seem to assume that, this being the case, it has now been sanctioned and legitimized by precedent.

But the fact is that it remains on the books as a prescription both of the laws of war and of international treaties to which we are parties; and none of this is changed by the fact that we ourselves liberally violated it thirty or forty years ago. And even if it were not thus prescribed by law and treaty, it should, as I see it, be prescribed by Christian conscience. For the resort to war is questionable enough from the Christian standpoint even in the best of circumstances; and those who, as believing Christians, take it upon their conscience to give the order for such slaughter (and I am not saying that there are never situations where this seems to be the lesser of the two evils)—those who do this owe it to their religious commitment to assure that the sufferings brought to innocent and helpless people by the military operations are held to the absolute minimum—and this, if necessary, even at the cost of military victory. For victory itself, even at its apparent best, is a questionable concept. I can think of no judgments of statesmanship in modern times where we have made greater mistakes, where the relationship between calculations and results have been more ironic, than those which related to the supposed glories of victory and the supposed horrors of defeat. Victory, as the consequences of recent wars have taught us, is ephemeral; but the killing of even one innocent child is an irremedial fact, the reality of which can never be eradicated.

Now the nuclear weapon offends against this principle as no other weapon has ever done. Other weapons can bring injury to noncombatants by accident or inadvertence or callous indifference; but they don't always have to do it. The nuclear weapon cannot help doing it, and doing it massively, even where the injury is unintended by those who unleash it.

Worse still, of course, and utterly unacceptable from the Christian standpoint as I see it, is the holding of innocent people hostage to the policies of their government, and the readiness, or the threat, to punish them as a means of punishing their government. Yet how many times—how many times just in these recent years—have we seen that possibility reflected in the deliberations of those who speculate and calculate about the possible uses of nuclear weapons? How many times have we had to listen to these terrible euphemisms about how many cities or industrial objects we would "take out" if a government did not do what we wanted it to do, as though what were involved here were only some sort of neat obliteration of an inanimate object, the removal of somebody else's pawn on the chessboard, and not, in all probability, the killing and mutilation of innocent people on a scale previously un-

known in modern times (unless it be, if you will, in the Holocaust of recent accursed memory)?

II

These things that I have been talking about are only those
qualities of the nuclear weapon which violate the traditional
limitations that were supposed to rest even upon the conduct
of conventional warfare. But there is another dimension to this
question that carries beyond anything even conceived of in the
past; and that is, of course, the possible, if not probable, effect
of nuclear warfare on the entire future of civilization—and, in
a sense, on its past as well. It has recently been forcefully
argued (and not least in Jonathan Schell's powerful book, *The
Fate of the Earth*, 1982) that not only would any extensive
employment of nuclear weapons put an end to the lives of
many millions of people now alive, but it would in all probability inflict such terrible damage to the ecology of the Northern
Hemisphere and possibly of the entire globe as simply to destroy the very capacity of our natural environment for sustain-
ing civilized life, and thus to put an end to humanity's past as
well as its future.

Only scientists are qualified, of course, to make final judgments on such matters. But we nonscientists are morally
bound, surely, to take into account not only the certain and
predictable effects of our actions but also the possible and
probable ones. Looking at it from this standpoint, I find it
impossible not to accept Schell's thesis that in even trifling
with the nuclear weapon, as we are now doing, we are placing
at risk the entire civilization of which we are a part.

Just think for a moment what this means. If we were to use
these devices in warfare, or if they were to be detonated on any
considerable scale by accident or misunderstanding, we might
be not only putting an end to civilization as we now know it
but also destroying the entire product of humanity's past
efforts in the development of civilized life, that product of
which we are the beneficiaries and without which our own lives
would have no meaning: the cities, the art, the learning, the

mastery of nature, the philosophy—what you will. And it would be not just the past of civilization that we were destroying; we would, by the same token, be denying to countless generations as yet unborn, denying to them in our unlimited pride and selfishness, the very privilege of leading a life on this earth, the privilege of which we ourselves have taken unquestioning and greedy advantage, as though it were something owed to us, something to be taken for granted, and something to be conceded or denied by us to those who might come after us—conceded or denied, as we, in our sovereign pleasure, might see fit.

How can anyone who recognizes the authority of Christ's teaching and example accept, even as a humble citizen, the slightest share of responsibility for doing this—and not just for doing it, but for even incurring the risk of doing it? This civilization we are talking about is not the property of our generation alone. We are not the proprietors of it; we are only the custodians. It is something infinitely greater and more important than we are. It is the whole; we are only a part. It is not our achievement; it is the achievement of others. We did not create it. We inherited it. It was bestowed upon us; and it was bestowed upon us with the implicit obligation to cherish it, to preserve it, to develop it, to pass it on—let us hope improved, but in any case intact—to the others who were supposed to come after us.

And this obligation, as I see it, is something more than just a secular one. The great spiritual and intellectual achievements of Western civilization: the art (including the immense Christian art), the architecture, the cathedrals, the poetry, the prose literature—these things were largely unthinkable without the faith and the vision that inspired them and the spiritual and intellectual discipline that made possible their completion. Even where they were not the products of a consciously experienced faith, how can they be regarded otherwise than as the workings of the divine spirit—the spirit of beauty and elevation and charity and harmony—the spirit of everything that is the opposite of meanness, ugliness, cynicism, and cruelty?

Must we not assume that the entire human condition out
of which all this has arisen—our own nature, the character of
the natural world that surrounds us, the mystery of the genera-
tional continuity that has shaped us, the entire environmental
framework, in other words, in which the human experiment
has proceeded—must we not assume that this was the framework in which God meant it to proceed—that this was the
house in which it was meant that we should live—that this was
the stage on which the human drama, our struggle out of
beastliness and savagery into something higher, was meant to
be enacted? Who are we, then, the actors, to take upon ourselves the responsibility of destroying this framework, or even
risking its destruction?

Included in this civilization we are so ready to place at risk
are the contributions of our own parents and grandparents—
of people we remember. These were, in many instances, humble contributions, but ones wrung by those people from trouble
and sacrifice, and all of them equal, the humble ones and the
momentous ones, in the sight of God. These contributions
were the products not just of our parents' efforts but of their
hopes and their faith. Where is the place for these efforts, these
hopes, that faith, in the morbid science of mutual destruction
that has so many devotees, official and private, in our country?
What becomes, in that mad welter of calculations about who
could take out whom, and how many millions might survive,
and how we might hope to save our own poor skins by digging
holes in the ground, and thus perhaps surviving into a world
not worth surviving into—what becomes in all this of the hopes
and the works of our own parents? Where is the place, here,
for the biblical injunction to "honor thy father and mother"
—that father and mother who stand for us not only as living
memories but as symbols of all the past out of which they, too,
arose, and without which their own lives, too, had no meaning?

I cannot help it. I hope I am not being unjust or uncharita-
ble. But to me, in the light of these considerations, the readiness to use nuclear weapons against other human beings—
against people whom we do not know, whom we have never
seen, and whose guilt or innocence it is not for us to establish

—and, in doing so, to place in jeopardy the natural structure upon which all civilization rests, as though the safety and the perceived interests of our own generation were more important than everything that has ever taken place or could take place in civilization: this is nothing less than a presumption, a blasphemy, an indignity—an indignity of monstrous dimensions—offered to God!

About the Author

George Frost Kennan was born in Milwaukee, Wisconsin, and educated at St. John's Military Academy and Princeton University. Entering the American Foreign Service in 1926, he was soon chosen for training as an expert on Soviet affairs. He served as Minister-Counselor in Moscow in 1944 and returned as Ambassador to the USSR in 1952. He served again as Ambassador to Yugoslavia from 1961 to 1963. Since 1953, with the exception of his years in Yugoslavia, Mr. Kennan has pursued a career as a scholar with the Institute for Advanced Study at Princeton, first as a Permanent Professor and, since 1974, as Professor Emeritus.

George Kennan has written some fifteen books, in addition to a large number of articles, most of them dealing with Russia and the Soviet Union. Two of these books—*Russia Leaves the War*, volume 1 of *Soviet-American Relations 1917–1920* (Princeton University Press, 1956) and *Memoirs 1925–1950* (Atlantic–Little, Brown, 1968) —have been honored both with the Pulitzer Prize and the National Book Award. He has received a number of other honors, including honorary degrees from Oxford, Harvard, Yale, and Princeton; the Albert Einstein Peace Prize (1981); and most recently, the peace prize of the German Booksellers Association (Frankfurt, 1982). Mr. Kennan has been, for many years, a member of the American Academy of Arts and Letters (serving as president of that academy from 1968–1972), and is currently co-chairman of the American Committee on East-West Accord.